EDITORIAL

Speaking over the noise

The news cycle has never felt as quick and urgent as in 2020. But crucial stories have gone under the radar, writes **Jemimah Steinfeld**

49(04): 1/3 | DOI: 10.1177/0306422020981248

CONSTANT REFRESHING OF news sites to see the latest infection rates; phones pinging with messages about lockdown; entire dinner conversations discussing when it will all end. Since the moment Chinese state media reported the first death from a novel coronavirus in mid-January, the whole world has been completely transfixed by Covid-19. And rightly so. At the time of writing the virus has killed more than 1.3 million people and wrought huge damage on our emotional and economic wellbeing, the extent of which will become only more evident as the months roll on. The media has been compelled to keep us all as informed as possible about a situation with such profound implications.

But all of this coverage has come at a cost. Journalists from all around newsrooms were conscripted, especially in the early days, to report on the pandemic, the stories they might otherwise have covered going unreported.

Then there are the financial troubles, plus the very real barriers to reporting that the closure of border has facilitated. Some journalists have been locked out of places they would normally cover; others have chosen to go home to avoid being away from loved ones for an indefinite period. Foreign reporting has been thrown into jeopardy. And with that once again non-Covid stories have been brushed under the rug.

All the while, our resolve to absorb these non-Covid stories has been weakened. Early stats said we consumed a lot more news. (There was initially a swell of traffic to news sites around the world, with broadcasters logging record ratings, including an uptick in younger viewers.) But as the crisis started to drag on, the numbers started to dwindle, at least within mainstream media. Covid fatigue set in. A study by the Pew Research Center at the end of April, for example, found that around seven in 10 Americans said they needed breaks from news about the pandemic. We headed over to Netflix instead.

A mixture of Covid fatigue and Covid distraction has fed into the hands of the world's dictators, who thrive on distraction, panic and confusion. They love noise. And that is precisely what the pandemic has given them.

Censorship is a multi-pronged tool; it can just as easily be a blunt knife, hacking away at stories without much subtlety, as a highlighter pen, bolding in yellow the parts it wants you to look at while your eyes skim over the other sections. With the media focused almost exclusively on one story, dictators have taken advantage to push through all kinds of measures that would otherwise cause outrage. As we →

EDITOR & HEAD OF CONTENT
Jemimah Steinfeld

SUB EDITORS
Tracey Bagshaw,
Adam Aiken

CONTRIBUTING EDITORS
Kaya Genç (Turkey),
Laura Silvia Battaglia
(Yemen and Iraq),
Stephen Woodman
(Mexico), Rachael Jolley
(UK and international)

EDITORIAL ASSISTANT
Benjamin Lynch

ART DIRECTOR
Matthew Hasteley

COVER
Ben Jennings

ASSOCIATE EDITOR
Mark Frary

MAGAZINE PRINTED BY
Page Bros.,
Norwich UK

INDEX ON CENSORSHIP
indexoncensorship.org | 1 Rivington Place, London EC2A 3BA, United Kingdom

reflect on the year, we want to make sure these stories are instead heard.

We want the world to know about a trio of laws that longstanding Nicaraguan leader Daniel Ortega is seeking to pass, which will destroy what little independent media is left. Nicaraguan human rights defender Bianca Jagger describes the situation in the country as harrowing. "We are witnessing a brutal repression of the media, the opposition, the students, the church," she said (p14).

Over in the Philippines, journalists continue to be murdered. We want the world to know their names. As part of a new series for the magazine, in which we will profile one person per issue who has recently been killed simply for exercising their free expression, we look at the life and death of Rex Cornelio (p18). He was shot dead in May while on his motorbike with his wife riding on the back. Cornelio frequently reported on land-rights issues in the country, in addition to corruption. In our long-read on who exactly he was, Rappler journalist Ryan Macasero talks to his widow and colleagues.

"You'd never hear him curse anyone, shout or get angry. He was brave, but a kind man. You could tell by the number of people who came out to his funeral. Many people told me about how Rex was always willing to help them out when they needed it," said his widow.

In Istanbul, Turkish contributing editor Kaya Genç talks to people who worked at a prominent university, Şehir University, which

was completely shut down overnight (p29). Imagine if the same happened to Cambridge or Columbia.

A new Chinese government policy to limit language instruction in Inner Mongolia has led to a series of suicides. People killing themselves for their language is unprecedented, writes Uradyn E Bulag (p49). Indeed it might be, though a crackdown by the Chinese government on its ethnic minorities is sadly not. Could this be the start of attacks on basic rights similar to those we have seen in Xinjiang and Tibet? If so, it's a story that deserves more attention.

A series of elections and political reshuffling have taken place with worrying outcomes. In Poland, the narrow victory of Andrzej Duda in presidential elections this July has given added weight to the leading party's conservative, right-wing agenda – something women and those in the LGBTQ community are now suffering the consequences of (p26). Our concerns are even greater in Slovenia, which until this year was considered liberal. It now has a leader who is a close ally of Hungarian prime minister Viktor Orban and is cut from the same cloth. "Like Orban, Janša's political campaigns have been based on xenophobia, Islamophobia and hate speech," writes Anuška Delić (p39). In Duda, Janša and Orban, we are watching the formation of a worrying axis in Europe, which might threaten the political balance of the bloc.

That is not to say all news stories have been under-reported. Global fury arose when the Chinese government forced a law on Hong Kong that makes any form of speech critical of Beijing punishable. Outside the special report, we ask academics, activists and politicians what we can and should be doing to support those who are suffering at the hands of the Chinese state (p61). And after years of silence on Xinjiang, people around the world are finally speaking out about what can only be called a genocide of the Uighur people. Nick Holdstock dives into the history of the region to explain

> *A mixture of Covid fatigue and Covid distraction has fed into the hands of the world's dictators, who thrive on distraction, panic and confusion. They love noise*

exactly what led to the current situation (p56), while in our culture section we publish poems from Uighur writers who have disappeared in the vast concentration camp network (p94).

Of course, one person who has not missed out in the 2020 news cycle is US President Donald Trump. Academic Robert Speel writes that the lead-up to and aftermath of November's election is not exceptional within US history, where lies and attacks have featured in other elections (p70). What can we learn, if anything?

Finally, I'd like to introduce two other new columns. The first will explore broader issues relating to free expression. In our opening one, the philosopher John Gray writes about John Stuart Mill, oft seen as the godfather of free expression, and asks whether some of the current divisions in society might be explained by looking more closely at Mill's life and work (p66). The second is a debate column kick-started by the most topical of themes – vaccine misinformation (p76). Two leading thinkers in the field of vaccinations, global health policy and misinformation go head-to-head to discuss whether social media sites should censor anti-vax posts, both from a moral perspective and in terms of outcomes. It's an illuminating read that will likely challenge many assumptions.

With that in mind, I would like to wish you all a very restful end of 2020. Here is hoping that 2021 is healthier and happier. ⊗

Jemimah Steinfeld *is head of content at Index*

CONTENTS

VOLUME 49 NUMBER 04 – WINTER 2020

1 SPEAKING OVER THE NOISE JEMIMAH STEINFELD
In a year where there has almost been too much news, we reflect on some of the most important stories

MASKED BY COVID
The underreported stories of 2020 that need to be heard

8 ANOTHER EXPLOSION FOR LEBANON
ZAHRA HANKIR, KAREEM CHEHAYEB
The blast in Beirut made international headlines. Even before that the nation was in turmoil and it has only worsened the mental health crisis

14 WHO WILL REPORT ON NICARAGUA?
JEMIMAH STEINFELD
Bianca Jagger tells Index a clampdown on dissent and independent media is reaching new heights

18 REMEMBERING REX CORNELIO RYAN MACASERO
Months on from the murder of Philippines radio host Rex Cornelio we speak to those who knew him about his bravery and his awful death

23 ROYALLY SILENCED PAVIN CHACHAVALPONGPUN
As students campaign against lèse-majesté laws, the Thai exile and royal critic with a Facebook group of two million followers considers their fate

26 ANOTHER BLACK DAY FOR POLAND
KATARZYNA KASIA
The attack on women's reproductive rights caused mass protests. Duda's re-election gave it legitimacy

29 TEARING DOWN THE IVORY TOWER KAYA GENÇ
Amidst the noise of the pandemic, a thriving Istanbul university was shut down with litle outcry

32 GANGING UP AGAINST THE TRUTH
CHRIS HAVLER-BARRETT
El Salvador's government do not want you to hear about a potential deal they've made with the country's biggest gang

36 MEXICO'S DEADLIEST STATE STEPHEN WOODMAN
The government's promise to protect journalists from harm is failing. Just look at the state of Veracruz

39 EUROPE'S NEW ORBAN ANUŠKA DELIĆ
Janez Janša, Slovenia's new prime minister, is mirroring the extreme policies of his Hungarian counterpart

42 DEMOCRACY VERSUS THE PEOPLE
ANDY MORGAN
Mali has seen a government coup following escalating protests. What has caused the unrest?

46 "THE STATE WON'T PROTECT YOU"
NATASHA JOSEPH
The death of Robert Mugabe brought so much hope, but improvements to daily life have not come for Zimbabweans. Far from it

49 DYING FOR THE MOTHER TONGUE URADYN E BULAG
Why have people in Inner Mongolia recently taken their lives?

52 HEY, BIG BROTHER – WE'RE WATCHING YOU RUTH SMEETH
We will fight louder and harder for those whose governments have taken away their freedoms

CREDIT:Ben Jennings

IN FOCUS

56 LONG MARCH TOWARDS CULTURAL GENOCIDE
NICK HOLDSTOCK

As news emerges of the present horrors happening in Xinjiang, an expert on the region looks at its recent history

61 HOW TO CHALLENGE CHINA TOM TUGENDHAT, LOKMAN TSUI, RUSHAN ABBAS, ANNE-MARIE BRADY

How do we make a global power sit up and take notice? These experts offer advice

64 ABUSE NOT PART OF JOURNALIST'S DAY JOB FRÉDERIKE GEERDINK

A reporter in the Netherlands has won a landmark case against her online harassers

66 TWO FACES OF ON LIBERTY JOHN GRAY

Liberal institutions are becoming more censorial. Is the philosopher John Stuart Mill to blame?

70 OUT WITH THE OLD? ROBERT SPEEL

Donald Trump's conduct during and after the election appeared extraordinary, but a look at US history challenges that

73 THE SUDANESE REVOLUTION WILL BE ILLUSTRATED ABRAHAM T ZERE

A profile of Khalid Albaih, the politcal cartoonist dubbed "an enemy of the state"

76 SOCIAL MEDIA PLATFORMS HAVE A MORAL DUTY TO BAN MISINFORMATION ABOUT VACCINES JONATHAN KENNEDY AND JULIE LEASK

Two leading thinkers on vaccine hesitancy and misinformation debate this crucial question

CULTURE

82 FIGHTING THE PROPAGANDA TSARS
SERGEY KHAZOV-CASSIA

The Russian writer speaks to Index about why his books are sold wrapped in plastic and shares an extract from The Gospel According To

87 BANNING THOSE WHO BAN BOTHAYNA AL-ESSA

Jemimah Steinfeld talks to the Kuwaiti author about a landmark case in the country that saw a ban on books overturned. Plus an exclusive extract from al-Essa's book Guardian of Superficialities

94 "YOUR LIMITLESS GRIEF IS A TALE WITH NO ENDING" JOSHUA L FREEMAN

We publish the poetry of three Uighur poets - Abuqadir Jüme Tunyuquq, Idris Nurillah and Shahip Abdusalam Nurbeg - who have disappeared in China

97 WORLD LOSES TITANS OF FREE SPEECH
BENJAMIN LYNCH

A look at the free speech advocates that recently passed away including Sir Harold Evans

100 PAGE TURNERS OR SLOW BURNERS?
LEAH CROSS, JESSICA NÍ MHAINÍN AND MARC NASH

New books reviewed on the murder of a Honduran activist, stories from a Tibetan town and a semi-autobiographical account of an artist in the USA

102 FIGHTING FOR COVID INFORMATION
LAUREN BROWN

Meet the people who are ensuring that even those in the most censored environments receive accurate information on the pandemic

---

CHIEF EXECUTIVE
Ruth Smeeth

EDITOR & HEAD OF CONTENT
Jemimah Steinfeld

FINANCE DIRECTOR
David Sewell

ASSOCIATE EDITOR
Mark Frary

SENIOR EVENTS
& PARTNERSHIPS MANAGER
Leah Cross

SENIOR POLICY RESEARCH
& ADVOCACY OFFICER
Jessica Ní Mhainín

EDITORIAL ASSISTANT
Benjamin Lynch

DIRECTORS & TRUSTEES
Trevor Phillips (Chair),
Anthony Barling,
Kate Maltby, Elaine Potter,
David Schlesinger,
Mark Stephens,
Kiri Kankhwende,
Sarah Sands

PATRONS
Margaret Atwood,
Simon Callow, Steve Coogan,
Brian Eno, Christopher Hird,
Lord Joel Joffe, Jude Kelly,
Michael Palin, Matthew Parris,
Alexandra Pringle,
Gabrielle Rifkind,
Sir Tom Stoppard,
Lady Sue Woodford Hollick

ADVISORY COMMITTEE
Julian Baggini,
Clemency Burton-Hill,
Ariel Dorfman, Michael Foley,
Andrew Franklin, Conor Gearty,
Andrew Graham-Yooll,
AC Grayling, Lyndsay Griffiths,
William Horsley,
Anthony Hudson,
Natalia Koliada, Jane Kramer,
Htein Lin, Jean-Paul Marthoz,
Robert McCrum,
Rebecca MacKinnon,
Beatrice Mtetwa, Julian Petley,
Michael Scammell,
Kamila Shamsie, Michael Smyth,
Tess Woodcraft, Christie Watson

MAIN: Anti-discrimination protesters march towards the Polish persidential palace in Warsaw in August, 2020

SPECIAL REPORT

≡ MASKED BY COVID: The underreported stories of 2020 that need to be heard

8	**ANOTHER EXPLOSION FOR LEBANON**	ZAHRA HANKIR, KAREEM CHEHAYEB
14	**WHO WILL REPORT ON NICARAGUA?**	JEMIMAH STEINFELD
18	**REMEMBERING REX CORNELIO**	RYAN MACASERO
23	**ROYALLY SILENCED**	PAVIN CHACHAVALPONGPUN
26	**ANOTHER BLACK DAY FOR POLAND**	KATARZYNA KASIA
29	**TEARING DOWN THE IVORY TOWER**	KAYA GENÇ
32	**GANGING UP AGAINST THE TRUTH**	CHRIS HAVLER-BARRETT
36	**MEXICO'S DEADLIEST STATE**	STEPHEN WOODMAN
39	**EUROPE'S NEW ORBAN**	ANUŠKA DELIĆ
42	**DEMOCRACY VERSUS THE PEOPLE**	ANDY MORGAN
46	**"THE STATE WON'T PROTECT YOU"**	NATASHA JOSEPH
49	**DYING FOR THE MOTHER TONGUE**	URADYN E BULAG

CREDIT: Piotr Lapinski/Getty

Another explosion for Lebanon

The Beirut blast, protests, an economy in freefall — all of this has deepened a mental health crisis in Lebanon. But it's not something people feel they can talk about, write **Zahra Hankir** and **Kareem Chehayeb**

49(04): 8/13 | DOI: 10.1177/0306422020981249

AT ABOUT FOUR in the afternoon on 4 August, Elie Halabi awoke from a deep slumber in his modest Beirut apartment in the deprived port neighbourhood of Medawar, Karantina. Shortly after the 62-year-old got up, his sister-in-law Claudette dropped by to offer him a home-cooked meal as usual. Elie, a soft-spoken, small man who lives alone and admits to constantly craving company, asked her if she could stay a little while longer. It was out of character for Claudette, 75, to turn down Elie's invitation. But she said she was tired and retreated to her first-floor apartment. Elie made himself a cup of Turkish coffee instead.

Within two hours, a massive explosion at the Port of Beirut, around the corner from Karantina, ripped through the Lebanese capital, levelling entire neighbourhoods and

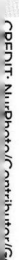

demolishing the three-storey building that Elie lived in and partly owned. The blast, triggered by 2,750 tonnes of improperly stored ammonium nitrate, claimed more than 200 lives, including Claudette's, and wounded more than 6,000 others. It also killed three of Elie's Syrian refugee neighbours: Khalidiya Hajj Steify, 40, and two of her daughters, Latifa, 22, and Joud, 12. About 300,000 people, including Elie, were left homeless following the explosion, which was one of the world's biggest non-nuclear blasts. It all but destroyed the area's hospitals and schools and plunged a country already in disarray into a humanitarian crisis.

Elie said that in addition to losing his sister-in-law and home that evening he also lost his peace of mind. While Lebanon's economic collapse, coupled with coronavirus

ABOVE: 24 days after the explosion, a man gazes out at the city in his damaged Beirut apartment

SPECIAL REPORT

→ restrictions, had weighed him down – he would sometimes deprive himself of luxuries such as bananas due to rising costs – Elie was content with what he had. It was the blast that finally broke him, precipitating a prolonged bout of depression and anxiety.

"I'm not sleeping at all. When I do sleep, I have nightmares in which I imagine everyone near me buried under debris and calling out for help," Elie told Index. "They needed me to help, but I couldn't move. It's like a video that's replaying in my head. I'm constantly reliving those moments. I sometimes wake up in the middle of the night, screaming their names. My wounds are psychological – I will never forget what I saw."

The incident also brought back painful memories from Lebanon's 15-year-long civil war.

A different crisis exposed

Lebanon is a nation in perpetual crisis: economically, politically and, less spoken about, psychologically.

Public health services in the country are insufficient and poorly funded; more than 80% of hospitals and healthcare facilities are private. Just one in 10 people in Lebanon with mental illnesses has access to the right care, and there are only two psychiatrists per 100,000 people. An economic meltdown prompted the government to cut healthcare spending by 7% earlier this year and private insurance companies don't cover psychotherapy – even though some experts say that's precisely what's needed the most.

"Living in Lebanon is a slow death," said Dayna Ash, a 31-year-old writer, feminist and activist who suffers from heightened anxiety. "I'm looking out of my window right now, and there's a hill of trash that's just appeared. Anxiety is a constant in this country. We've got to a point where we've normalised it. I just don't see past tomorrow."

In the period between the blast and the end of September, Embrace – a Beirut-based non-profit organisation focusing on mental health awareness – said it received 1,200 calls to its emotional support and suicide prevention lifeline. That compares with 1,000 calls in the first nine months of 2019. About 20% of the callers said the explosion and its impact on them was among the main reasons they were seeking assistance.

"The blast destroyed so many of us on a different level," Hiba Dandachli, a board member and communications adviser at Embrace, said. "We all lost something that day."

Even before the explosion, the mental health crisis was worsening. So far in 2020, the total number of calls logged by Embrace has risen by 300%, partly due to the deteriorating socioeconomic situation and the pandemic, which necessitated lockdowns across the country and burdened the already ailing healthcare system.

Over the past two years, a spate of suicides has rattled the nation. In February 2019, one man set himself on fire in front of a private school after failing to pay his daughter's fees. In July, a man shot himself in a busy Beirut district after leaving a note suggesting hunger was his impetus. Psychiatrists and medics have warned of a national mental health epidemic, which is expected to deepen as the country's economic and political fallout intensifies.

Racha Hijazi, a Sidon-based licensed clinical psychologist and cognitive-behavioural therapist, said the combination of these factors had caused a spike in anxiety across the country, with many of her patients saying that the very act of survival can feel insurmountable.

"People are drowning in anxiety," she said. "Their anxiety has reached a point where their lives have become dysfunctional. Whenever there is another explosion or fire in Lebanon, you drag people back into the grief process. You're not allowing them to heal. People are going to suffer for a long time."

Hijazi said she had seen an increase in bouts of memory loss, lack of concentration and exhaustion, as well as other cognitive-behavioural changes related to trauma.

Stigma across borders

Lebanon is certainly not alone. Middle East and North African countries have seen some of the highest rates of depression anywhere in the world – in part due to the lack of stability triggered by war and rapid urbanisation. Women are disproportionately affected and resources

for prospective patients are scant, with governments allocating little to mental health budgets, if anything at all. The stigma accompanying mental illness in the region remains pervasive, despite some strides forward.

Wishing to be referred to just as Samah, a 32-year-old aid worker who survived the blast, said her mental health had become more of a priority over the past 12 months as she had struggled to process the trauma she'd witnessed and endured in the field.

"Growing up as an Arab, discussing mental health issues is stigmatised. It's often seen as you're 'disturbed' somehow, or you need dramatic psychiatric care," she said. "It was very much a taboo topic growing up in my household and community."

The older generation's method of coping with tragedy focused on the physical rather than the emotional or psychological, she added.

That said, the economic situation has proven to be a bigger barrier than stigma, according to Rima Makki, a mental health activity manager for Doctors Without Borders in Lebanon.

"We're receiving calls from people who were well-off and had the means to do therapy but now can't continue treatment."

Lebanon's economy has continued to spiral after a dollar shortage in September 2019 wreaked panic and havoc at banks. A protest in central Beirut a few weeks later sparked a countrywide uprising against the ruling elite, calling for structural changes and an end to decades of corruption. The economic impact of Covid-19 later spurred another devastating blow. In less than 12 months, Lebanon's currency lost 80% of its value, with unemployment and food prices simultaneously rocketing. Prior to the explosion, the UN revealed that more than half the population was living in poverty. The blast also ravaged the country's key grain silo, compounding Lebanon's food security crisis.

And there is no viable social safety net or pension scheme in Lebanon to mitigate the economic crash's impact.

"People are not just reacting to the explosion itself but to years of systematic oppression that have much deeper mental health consequences,"

Whenever there is another explosion or fire in Lebanon, you drag people back into the grief process. You're not allowing them to heal. People are going to suffer for a long time

said Nawal Muradwij, a clinician-in-training at City University New York.

Looking at the narrative around trauma, she said there had been a rejection of the idea that Lebanese people were resilient as "it diverts focus away from the oppressive context in which these mental health considerations take place".

NGOs and the media play a part

Where the government has failed, non-governmental organisations have stepped up – a phenomenon witnessed acutely in the aftermath of the explosion. Local and international civil society organisations, along with mental health experts, have spent years prioritising funding for mental illness, policy changes and improving community attitudes. Following the explosion, Embrace and other non-profits joined a coalition called Basecamp to assist with relief efforts, offering emotional support services.

Psychologists and psychiatrists, including Hijazi, have banded together to provide services to the underprivileged for free. And Haven for Artists, which is based in Achrafiyeh, one of the neighbourhoods that was hit by the blast, transformed its premises into a shelter and organised free mental health sessions and drama and art therapy. Embrace has also seen a surge in the number of volunteers wanting to help with relief efforts, according to Dandachli.

Mental illness has been on the country's radar for the past decade, although implementation has been slow and reliant on partners in the humanitarian sector. In 2014, Lebanon's health ministry, in co-operation with the International Medical Corps and the World Health Organization, announced a National Mental Health Programme which was designed to →

ABOVE: Activities for young children affected by the blast are organised by volunteers

→ "reform mental healthcare in Lebanon, and provide services beyond medical treatment at the community level".

In 2015, a five-year plan was released, detailing structural reforms at the ministry, legislative changes, funding mechanisms and a communications and advocacy strategy, to scale up services and awareness campaigns. But much remains to be done.

Hijazi believes the media can perpetuate anxiety by repeatedly airing footage that "recreates trauma over and over again", as well as provoking vicarious trauma in those who haven't experienced catastrophic events first-hand.

But some have helped by prioritising mental health messaging. Broadcasters such as LBC and MTV have hosted psychiatrists and tackled mental illness on popular television shows. The shift in attitudes is starting to take hold, according to Samah, in part because the situation in Lebanon has become so unbearable that the Millennial and Gen-Z generations simply can't overlook mental health, given they are continually experiencing crippling anxiety.

"Our generation is far more open to speaking about these issues [than] my parents' generation," she said.

Old habits die hard

While the stigma has lessened among the younger generations, the middle-aged and elderly often refuse professional help as they've developed mechanisms by which they attempt to deal with trauma by themselves. For example, Elie Halabi refuses to see a psychiatrist, in part due to how people have responded to him when he shows "weakness".

"I have depression. But I've never talked about this with anyone, and I don't want to, because I know what they'd say: 'Pull yourself together'," he said.

"That's what they say, or they mock or pity me. This isn't gymnastics. Why would I need to pull myself together? It's my mind that is troubled."

Instead, he said, he "puts his faith in God, the best medicine". He added: "Who else can I go to, anyway? I just want to survive. All I can think about is tomorrow."

Hijazi traces the spike in national anxiety levels back to the start of the October 2019 revolution, which led to the overthrow of prime minister Saad Hariri (who returned to office this October).

"The revolution was anxiety-provoking for many. It was as if people suddenly started to

CREDIT: Mohamed Azakir/Reuters

look around and say, 'Maybe my life is not as it should be'." Feelings of hopelessness have consumed people living in Lebanon to the extent that hundreds have attempted to flee the country in boats, risking their lives to make a treacherous journey by sea from Tripoli to Cyprus.

Given the country's outlook is bleak, with basic food prices projected to climb as the central bank is poised to end subsidies on goods including fuel, wheat and medicine in the coming weeks, Hijazi said people were focused on survival.

"When you're thinking, 'Am I going to be able to put food on the table for my family tomorrow?' or 'Can I pay my child's tuition fees or not?' you don't have the chance or the luxury to process your emotions," she said.

While some experts are optimistic about shifting attitudes, they point to limited access to medication due to the economic slump as a significant concern. Pharmacies have already started to report a shortage of drugs, with long queues forming amid panic buying and pharmacist strikes.

And the impact is being felt, according to Sabine Tawk of Skoun, which offers outpatient support to drug users. While the group hasn't witnessed a significant rise in substance use, Tawk said more than half of its clients had contended with job losses, salary cuts, food shortages and difficulty paying for medication. She said patients had reduced their prescribed doses which had, in turn, exacerbated anxiety and depression and the risk of relapse.

The mental health emergency is vast, impacting different people in myriad ways. Health care professionals have themselves had to contend with vicarious trauma. In the two weeks following the blast, Hijazi couldn't make any appointments as she struggled to overcome the shock herself. "If I want to help you, I have to help myself first," she said.

Meanwhile, vulnerable communities, among them Syrian and Palestinian refugees and the LGBTQ community, are also in great need. While some non-profits target these particular groups, many minorities still do not have the same resources or access as others. "Mar Mikhael and Gemmayze [areas left in ruins by

> *"Living in Lebanon is a slow death," said Dayna Ash, a 31-year-old writer, feminist and activist who suffers from heightened anxiety*

the blast] were considered a safe space for the LGBT community," said Ash, who is also the head of Haven for Artists. "Many of them live, frequent or work there. They came here as a way of life to avoid discrimination or physical abuse. That safe space has been destroyed."

Young people in particular have been severely affected, according to Unicef, with 50% of children showing signs of trauma. Pascale Safadi, who lost her home in Karantina on 4 August, said her four-year-old son and five-year-old daughter were deeply affected.

"We can't sleep at night," Safadi, 34, said. "As soon as it starts to get dark, my daughter starts crying and says, 'Mama, why did this happen to us? Why did they destroy our home?'"

Since then, her daughter, who was severely injured in the blast – the cause of which is still being investigated by the government – has talked about what she experienced only by pretending to be a journalist and asking her brother questions about the blast with a toy microphone. Safadi said she spoke to a psychiatrist about her children's situation and was advised to give them time to settle as they recovered from the acute stress associated with primary emotional triggers.

"Children need answers," Hijazi said. "You can't just say 'We don't know how this happened'." ⊗

Zahra Hankir and **Kareem Chehayeb** *are independent journalists based between Beirut, London and New York*

Who will report on Nicaragua?

With elections approaching, the president of Nicaragua has introduced a set of bills designed to muzzle what independent media remains. **Jemimah Steinfeld** talks to **Bianca Jagger** about the dire situation

A ONCE REVOLUTIONARY FIGURE, Nicaraguan president Daniel Ortega now resembles Anastasio Somoza, the dictator he helped overthrow 41 years ago. The country's leader between 1979 and 1990 and again since 2007, Ortega's most recent period in power has seen a brutal clampdown on dissent. The situation has become much worse since protests shook the country in 2018, and now the last free media outlet that can bear witness to these attacks – television station Canal 12 – is facing closure following a ruling that it has to pay the equivalent of about $600,000 in overdue taxes.

"Ortega is waging a relentless and savage persecution of journalists and independent media in Nicaragua," said Bianca Jagger, founder and president of the Bianca Jagger Human Rights Foundation, in an interview with Index.

Jagger, one of the most prominent voices against the government, was in Nicaragua in 2018 to support the release of the Amnesty International report on Ortega's shoot-to-kill policy of repression. The trip was far from peaceful as it happened at the same time as the aforementioned protests were rocking the country. They erupted over since-scrapped planned cuts to welfare benefits and later spread into broader protests against Ortega's increasingly authoritarian rule. Police and paramilitary groups (*turbas sandinistas*) crushed the protests, killing hundreds, injuring thousands and forcing thousands to flee the country.

Jagger witnessed first-hand the brutality of the police and the death squads when she participated in one of the largest demonstrations in Nicaragua at the time, on 30 May – Mother's Day. At least 11 people were killed and 79 were injured and, today, the situation has worsened so much that she would not risk going to the country.

"He would kill me," she said of Ortega, who she describes as a "murderous, brutal dictator".

"It is a harrowing situation in Nicaragua. We are witnessing a brutal repression of the media, the opposition, the students, the church. There continue to be executions of poor farmers, and members of the opposition and young people are put in jail."

Jagger speaks of "heinous" sexual violence used as torture and also says farmers are being executed in remote regions with few people knowing anything about it.

"Ortega not only has his army, he has his police, his riot police, and he has his death squad," she said.

With few NGOs and media networks now operating, those who are calling the government out on its crimes are few and far between. This makes the attack on Canal 12 all the worse.

The attacks on the media have come from all angles and journalists work in an increasingly hostile environment. Death threats, arbitrary arrests and harassment campaigns are commonplace. This situation became bad during Ortega's re-election in 2016, which saw him go after critical media, and then worse following the protests of 2018. Journalists could not cover the protests safely as they were seen as participants and were (and still are) denied the normal press safeguards. Most could not afford bulletproof vests and other equipment necessary to protect them. One reporter, Ángel Gahona, was shot dead while live-streaming the protests.

The dangers don't lie just in covering protests. Some journalists have been arrested and jailed on terrorism charges, such as Miguel

CREDIT: INTI OCON/AFP/Getty

Mora and Lucía Pineda Ubau, the latter of whom reported on corruption and allegations that Ortega had sexually assaulted his stepdaughter.

But there are other ways the government has been working to silence the media. Shortages of newsprint, for example, have pretty much wiped out printed newspapers, including the daily El Nuevo Diario, which had been in circulation since 1980. Television stations have been blocked; critical radio station Radio Darío was torched; and the government continues to confiscate journalists' equipment.

Then, in October, a "foreign agents" bill was passed that would allow Ortega's government to exert control over the work of virtually anyone who received funding or support from abroad, including rights groups and independent media outlets. At a similar time, pro-government lawmakers introduced a "cybercrime" bill, criminalising the spread of "fake news" and other speech on the internet. Ortega has also recently proposed a "hate speech law", which he threatened to use against government opponents. If passed, it would allow sentences of life in prison.

Many believe these bills are part of a strategy designed to crush opposition ahead of next year's elections. The Nicaraguan Independent Press Forum said in a statement that the cybercrimes bill was intended to "control and censure information on the internet, the only space for free communication that the dictators cannot dominate", while José Miguel Vivanco,

ABOVE: A student graffitis on the campus of the Central American University in Managua, November 2019

Americas director at Human Rights Watch, said: "These bills appear designed to provide legal cover for the Ortega government to harass and prosecute journalists, rights groups and virtually anyone who criticises his government."

All of this comes at a critical time in Nicaragua. In addition to the elections next year, the country is facing a worsening economic crisis. Added to this mix is the response to the Covid-19 pandemic. Official reports place the number of cases as being far lower than they are believed to be and, as a result, the government is encouraging people to go to mass →

Ortega not only has his army, he has his police, his riot police, and he has his death squad

ATTACKED FROM ALL ANGLES

All means to silence the media are used in Nicaragua, as BENJAMIN LYNCH shows in these examples

SINCE 1992, THREE journalists have been killed in Nicaragua, which sits 117th out of 180 countries in the Reporters Without Borders World Press Freedom Index 2020 (three places down from last year).

Prominent newspaper Confidencial was raided in 2018 and equipment including laptops were seized by armed police.

In October 2018, freelance journalist Carl David Goette-Luciak was criticised online for his coverage of anti-government protests before the authorities successfully sought to deport him for it. Earlier that year, Brazilian documentary maker Emilia Mello was arrested whilst trying to film a demonstration. She was subsequently deported.

TV channel 100% Noticias was ordered off the air and two of its journalists, Miguel Mora and Lucía Pineda, were arrested on terrorism charges and for "inciting violence" in April 2018. They were subsequently released.

In 2019, TV journalist Suyen Cortez was shopping with her daughter when she was approached and assaulted by a university professor with strong links to pro-government figures.

In March 2020, at the funeral of priest and writer Ernesto Cardenal, journalists were attacked by supporters of Daniel Ortega. Police were accused of "standing idly by" while reporters were targeted by the group.

But the deaths of journalists are not a new development. In June 1979, US journalist Bill Stewart was travelling in a clearly marked press vehicle and was shot dead by government forces at a roadblock.

→ gatherings of all kinds, schools to stay open and doctors to wear minimal protective gear.

"Many doctors are risking their lives," said Jagger, who added that over 100 doctors and health care workers had died as a result.

For many in Nicaragua, the assaults remind them of the dark days of the 1970s under the Somoza dictatorship.

"The Ortega regime is worse than Somoza in many ways," Jagger said. "It is worse because Daniel Ortega is killing children, students, women, the media, and he is persecuting the church."

One reporter, Ángel Gahona, was shot dead while live-streaming the protests

The attacks on Catholics in particular represent a break from the dictatorship of Somoza. The Catholic Church has historically played a powerful role in the country, but under Ortega bishops have been targeted for their support of protesters, while churches have been desecrated, including the recent burning of a cathedral housing a widely venerated crucifix.

Why has the world not paid more attention to these crimes? The distraction caused by Covid-19 is one reason, but Jagger believes there is more to it.

"The British media have given very little attention to Nicaragua, which has been quite shocking to me," she said. "I believe that because it is not a former British colony it is simply not high up on the British agenda." She says the French, American, Latin American and Spanish media have given the country far more attention.

Earlier this year, the USA also imposed sanctions on the Nicaraguan National Police over accusations of human rights abuses.

As for Nicaraguans themselves, while some continue to protest, others are less vocal and active. It's not just that they fear the current brutality, it is that they fear what could come next.

"As a student I campaigned against Somoza. Daniel Ortega is far worse," said Jagger. "Ortega was among the leaders of the revolution, but he betrayed the revolution and that's one of the reasons the people of Nicaragua are not ready anymore to embark upon an armed revolution. They know what happens – you get rid of one dictator to be replaced with another one."

Jemimah Steinfeld is head of content at Index

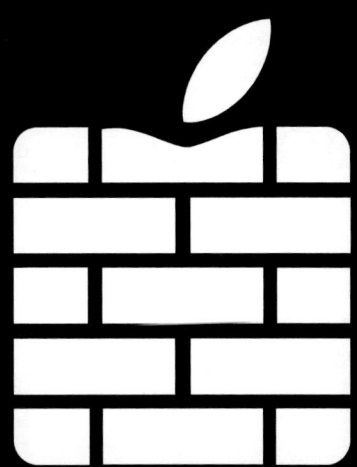

One Less Thing.

Apple censors over 3000 apps in its App Store. Soon there will be two kinds of people: those who can access uncensored information, and those who use Apple.

applecensorship.com

Remembering Rex Cornelio

Five months after his murder, there has been no justice for Philippine radio journalist Rex Cornelio. **Ryan Macasero** talks to those close to him about who he was and what his death means

49(04): 18/22 | DOI: 10.1177/0306422020981251

ON NEGROS ISLAND, gun violence is a part of life. But for most of the Covid-19 pandemic, it seemed to have been put on lockdown along with everything else. With its number of coronavirus cases under control, the lockdown in the Central Visayas island ended on 1 May. Checkpoints eased and people were allowed to go out again. And it seems this was the opportunity those who had been threatening radio journalist Cornelio Pepino – known as Rex Cornelio – had been looking for.

"He had been receiving threats in the days leading up to the shooting," Rex's wife, Coleen Pepino, said in a phone interview.

Cornelio was shot five times by gunmen on motorcycles on 6 May. Pepino, who was riding on the back of his motorbike, was unharmed.

In its October report, the Committee to Protect Journalists named the Philippines the seventh most dangerous place for journalists in the world, based on the number of killings of media workers that remain unsolved. Almost six months after the killing, Cornelio's case is still one of those.

Cornelio was the third radio journalist to be killed in the province of Negros Oriental since 2018. A murder in November of another journalist – Virgilio Maganes – has placed the total number of journalists killed so far under the administration of President Rodrigo Duterte at 18, according to the National Union of Journalists of the Philippines. Duterte is known for his attacks on the media; he said early in his term that being a journalist "does not exempt one from assassination" and calls critical journalists "fake news" (see Index issue 48(04) pp.33-35).

According to the tally by the NUJP, Cornelio was the 186th journalist killed since the fall of dictator Ferdinand Marcos in 1986.

Earlier on the same afternoon that Cornelio was shot dead, the Philippine congress denied the franchise of the country's biggest broadcast network ABS-CBN, a promise Duterte made shortly after he assumed office in 2016 due to the critical reporting of its news department.

Cornelio had been a radio reporter for 20 years, focusing his coverage on corruption, governance and environmental issues in Negros Oriental.

Going the extra mile

Energy FM 93.7 station manager Florence Baesa, Cornelio's boss, said he was meticulous in his reporting. "All of his reporting was factual," she said. "And he'd always go the extra mile to verify his sources – even going all the way to Cebu to check documents on environmental compliance of projects in the province."

According to Baesa, Cornelio's integrity and courage to pursue stories no others were pursuing would often get him in trouble. In 2015, for example, Cornelio was sued for libel by Negros Oriental governor Roel Degamo for his coverage of illegal gold mining in Santa Catalina town. The case was dismissed by a local judge in 2017.

The Dumaguete Post quoted judge Catherine Dato as saying: "The prosecution must understand that in criminal libel, the imputation of a crime, a vice or defect must be plainly clear and categorical, and cannot be left to presumptions, conjectures, inferences, guesswork or surmises."

Baesa said that the judge's dismissal of the case was a testament to Cornelio's work ethic.

For as long as there are good people, there is hope

"Everything he reported on and did on his editorial shows were based on facts," she said. In the case filed by Degamo, the judge also considered that Rex went to get Degamo's side of the story and waited for him all day outside his office, but got no answers.

Coleen Pepino said, however, that while radio commentators often got in trouble for emotionally charged commentaries, Rex – who did both editorials and straight news – was always calm and stuck to asking questions and basing his opinion on facts.

"You'd never hear him curse anyone, shout or get angry," she said. "He was brave, but a kind man. You could tell by the number of people who came out to his funeral. Many people told me about how Rex was always willing to help them out when they needed it."

His widow is left with three children and without employment, getting by only with the help of friends and family.

"My daughter cries when I'm not around. I've been crying a lot at night, but I try to stay strong for my children," Coleen said.

Lately, she said, her crying was for justice, which is often elusive in the Philippines.

Awaiting protection – and justice

In July 2020, the presidential taskforce on media security took over the investigation to avoid conflict as one of Degamo's security aides – police officer Ruel Piñero – was himself named a person of interest in the investigation. This was a taskforce created by the Duterte administration in 2016 for the protection of journalists and to investigate killings of media workers in the Philippines.

The investigation is still pending and Piñero remains on active duty.

The killings of two other radio journalists in Dumaguete City had also not yet been solved at the time of writing. Dindo Generoso was killed in November 2019 while Edumund Sestoso was shot dead in April 2018.

Violence has been a perennial struggle for everyone on the island and this is the very reason journalists who cover the social unrest are often caught in the crossfire of conflicts between landlords, organised workers and the insurgency, in addition to dealing with corruption and governance issues.

Both Negros Oriental and the neighbouring Negros Occidental, which are mainly agricultural economies, are consistently on the list of the 10 poorest Philippine provinces. This environment makes the island ripe for violence.

In 1986, Roman Catholic Bishop Antonio Fortich was quoted in The Washington Post calling the island a "social volcano" due to the violence caused by poverty.

"If this is not well handled, this will be the first province to explode," Fortich said in the report. Not much has changed on the island since then.

Despite efforts by government and non-government organisations to create mechanisms to protect journalists who face harassment and threats – and justice for those who are killed – journalists who become victims of violence hardly ever see convictions, according to the NUJP.

Its Bacolod City chapter president, Marchel Espina, knows of the dangers journalists face in Negros all too well.

From 2018 to 2019, due to intensified "anti-insurgency" operations, the island saw increased killings of farmers, activists and labour leaders.

Espina, who was a reporter for the Visayan Daily Star as well as Rappler, had a close encounter herself while covering a string of murders on the island. In the last week of July 2019, she tallied 15 riding-in-tandem killings (murders carried out by killers on motorbikes) and →

ABOVE: Radio journalist Rex Cornelio, who was shot on his motorbike by gunmen on 6 May

OPPOSITE: On International Human Rights Day in Manila, 2018, a protester covers herself in red dye to protest for land rights, something Cornelio covered in his writing

told Index: "I was tailed by unidentified men for pursuing this story on my way back to Bacolod from another town."

She added: "Intel officers sometimes take photos of journalists who attend press freedom rallies. Many of them are often red-tagged or are accused of being part of the communist party and its armed wing, the New People's Army."

The NUJP has been advocating for the safety of journalists – and accountability for those who threaten or attack journalists – since it was established in 2005. But justice moves slowly in the Philippines.

It took a decade, for example, for the courts to convict Zaldy and Andal Ampatuan for a 2009 massacre in which 32 journalists were among 58 people killed in one of the worst political killings in recent Philippine history.

But Cornelio's family and friends are hopeful that the police and courts will do the right thing in his case.

"I saw that there are people who are still doing the right and just thing," Coleen said in a press conference in August. Her shirt read, "You can silence this voice, but this message will make noise".

She added: "My husband decided to be good, for what is right. I accepted it and supported it."

And she encouraged others to do the same, saying: "I hope that you would tell your loved ones to do the right thing as well."

Non-stop threats

In the 20 years that Baesa knew Cornelio, she said that there was always someone angry about his work, and he had become accustomed to local officials passively or directly threatening his life. Cornelio was relentless in his pursuit of environment stories and local governance.

His stories made an impact, including his

CREDIT: Bullit Marquez/AP/Shutterstock

If I shut up every time someone gets angry, what will happen?

SPECIAL REPORT

I tell my reporters 'Don't be afraid'. We have to pray and be careful and get all sides. But if we don't do it, who will?

→ exposés leading to potentially destructive quarrying and mining projects being halted by the national government.

In 2019, watchdog Global Witness said that the Philippines was the most dangerous place to be an environmental activist, with at least 113 people killed under the Duterte administration. About 27% of these killings were of people who protested mining projects.

Because the threats had intensified, Cornelio had a police escort assigned to him – an escort he asked to stop following him a week before he was killed.

"He didn't like that police officers had to follow him everywhere and felt bad for them when he was doing his work," Coleen said. "He was brave. I had asked him if he could stop. 'What about me?' I asked him."

Coleen said he told her, "If this is God's will, then we have to accept it", and a week before he was killed, he warned Baesa, "If something happens to me, you know who did it", alluding to a politician Rex covered in the province.

Investigation hits a wall

Even though Duterte's media taskforce has taken over the investigation, Baesa believes it is still moving too slowly because "big" and "powerful" people are involved.

The police officer Piñero disappeared for several days in August, later turning up more than 160 kilometres away in Cebu City after his wife filed a writ of habeas corpus to locate him. Police said he was en route to a reassignment in Metro Manila, pending the investigation to see if he was involved in Cornelio's killing.

This is a common practice of the Duterte administration. Police officers are often reshuffled to other departments or assigned to other areas if accused of misconduct, committing a crime or being involved in drugs or corruption.

The taskforce has yet to determine if Piñero was involved, and it does not have substantial information on who killed Cornelio.

But despite the grim odds, Coleen has not given up hope that justice will be served for her husband.

"For as long as there are good people, there is hope," she said. "Those in power, they won't be in power forever. And whatever wrong they do, it will come back to them."

Journalism must continue

Baesa, who also strings for Cebu-based media outlets alongside managing the radio station, is working from home due to threats to her security.

"It was always the two of us who were willing to pursue the stories that hold our local elected officials accountable," she said. "For now, they advised that I should not go to the [radio] station because that's a security vulnerability."

But in an environment where corruption is rampant and accountability from public officials lacking, the veteran journalist said the threats would not stop her from doing her work.

"We were partners in a lot of the stories we pursued. We'd get documents, do the research, get the news."

Right now she is managing four reporters who are also chasing stories on local governance, the environment and other issues, on top of the ongoing Covid-19 pandemic.

"I tell my reporters 'Don't be afraid'. We have to pray and be careful and get all sides. But if we don't do it, who will?" she said.

Baesa said that despite the continuing threats to her own safety, she cannot – and will not – stop pursuing accountability stories from local officials.

"I'll continue doing it ethically – professionally. If someone gets angry or hurt by what we do, I can't do anything about that. If I shut up every time someone gets angry, what will happen?" ⊗

Ryan Macasero *is a reporter for Rappler based in the Philippines*

Royally silenced

Pavin Chachavalpongpun, whose Facebook group critical of the Thai monarchy has over two million members, considers what might happen to the country's student protesters

49(04): 23/25 | DOI: 10.1177/0306422020981252

IN THAILAND, CENSORSHIP has reached an alarming level whereby criticism against the country's most powerful political institution – the monarchy – is mercilessly penalised by a lengthy prison term, under the draconian lèse-majesté law. Issues related to the monarchy are traditionally considered sensitive. In particular, controversies surrounding the royal family are treated strictly as taboo. In dealing with this, the Thai state adopts two approaches: preventive and punitive, through censorship and the lèse-majesté law respectively.

Currently, Thailand has the harshest punishment for lèse-majesté violations in the world. Lèse-majesté, or the crime of injury to royalty, is defined by Article 112 of the Thai Criminal Code, which states that defamatory, insulting or threatening comments about the king, the queen and the regent are punishable by between three and 15 years in prison. The law allows anyone to file a complaint against others for insulting the monarchy.

Lèse-majesté, which came into law in Thailand in 1908, was initially a "weapon of choice" among the political elites to undermine their opponents. But almost 100 years later, after the 2006 coup, the arbitrary use of the law has proliferated among ordinary citizens. As the monarchy has become increasingly divisive, where people stand on the monarchy is often how they define themselves politically. As a result, use of the lèse-majesté law can come from all angles. An elder brother filed a complaint against his younger brother. A boss threatened to take his employer to court. From elites' retribution to personal revenge, the monarchy has been dangerously politicised by the lèse-majesté law.

While teaching in Kyoto, I was charged with lèse-majesté in the aftermath of the 2014 coup for being critical of the monarchy. Once accused, there followed a barrage of state harassment, from having a warrant issued for my arrest to having my Thai passport revoked, forcing me to apply for refugee status in Japan. The same tactic is now being employed against student protesters who are calling for immediate monarchical reform. This year has seen some of the largest protests calling for reform in Thailand's history. The government has threatened to arrest the protest leaders should they insist on their demands. The threat is interpreted as a form of state censorship against the protesters.

Today, the government is waging the war both physically and in cyberspace. While the lèse-majesté law is implemented to suppress the protesters on the streets, the Computer Crime Act – the latest censorship instrument – is exercised against online criticism of the monarchy.

What is the essence of the monarchical reform? The students are striving to constitutionalise the monarchy. Thailand abolished its absolute monarchy in 1932 and formally embraced a constitutional monarchy. But in the 88 years since, the monarchy has not adhered to this framework. King Bhumibol Adulyadej (1946-2016) operated outside the constitution, yet his operation was explained away as constitutional. His son, the current King Vajiralongkorn, further obscured the →

There followed a barrage of state harassment, from having a warrant issued for my arrest to having my Thai passport revoked

ABOVE: A pro-democracy protester wearing a fake crown and a shirt that reads "Please realise this country belongs to the people" during an anti-government rally in Bangkok, September 2020

→ line of royal prerogatives through his direct interventions in politics, ultimately for the augmentation of his own power. He is allowed to have his own military unit. He requested the amendment of the constitution in relation to royal power. He transferred all assets under the Crown Property Bureau to be under his sole possession, estimated at being worth at least $30 billion. The overwhelming power imbued in Vajiralongkorn is accompanied by his own notorieties as a playboy and an eccentric.

The students crafted a 10-point demand for the monarchy, including separating the king's personal property from the Crown Property Bureau; an end to the palace's intervention in politics; abolishing the military units under the direct demand of the palace; obliterating state propaganda on the monarchy; and investigating the abductions and killings of Thai activists overseas.

The students' 10-point demand sent shockwaves through the Thai state. Not only have the students attempted to diminish the royal prerogatives, they have also trespassed the limit of the lèse-majesté law. The growing confidence of the students comes down to the growing number of supporters who are rooting for their cause. The supporters have congregated

through online mobilisation under a private Facebook group, the Royalists Marketplace (RP). In April 2020, I set up the RP as a platform for serious discussion on the monarchy in an effort to dismantle the long-held taboo. Within four months of its inception, the number of members passed one million, suddenly posing a menace to the monarchy. The RP is successful because it has introduced myriad critical subjects related to the monarchy, including the political intervention of the king, the intimate relationship between the monarchy and the military, the super-rich status of the crown, and the maltreatment of anti-monarchist activists outside Thailand. The RP also created an environment of like-minded people, once intimidated because of their curiosity about the monarchy but who are now more confident in the company of other critics of the royal institution. The twin forces behind the students – on the streets and in the RP – together powerfully propelled the demand for monarchical reform to become a public agenda.

The state's responses to the students are, as expected, non-compromising. Lèse-majesté law still exists and functions well. Besides, the government relies on the Computer Crime Act to curb online criticism against the monarchy. That law defines computer crime offences and computer-related cybercrime, preventing anyone from criticising certain institutions deemed important to national security, some of which involved lèse-majesté. Critical comments against the monarchy are discursively translated into "false data", hence violating the Computer Crime Act. The exploitation of both

The students' 10-point demand sent shockwaves through the Thai state

the lèse-majesté law and the act has generated a huge impact on the student movement. Its leaders have been accused of violating the two laws, and it might be only a matter of time until widespread arrests take place. Should that happen, it could disrupt the protests.

As for the RP, the government was initially successful in requesting Facebook to block the group's access in Thailand. However, in less than 24 hours, Facebook shifted its position by suing the government for its illegitimate request. Facebook may have taken into consideration the cost-benefit aspect of the blocking. More essentially, Facebook signalled its upholding of the principle of freedom of expression and rejection of the forced censorship ordered by the Thai state. Facebook realised that failing to do so could encourage the thriving practice of state censorship. This case is ongoing. In the interim, if access to the page gets blocked again, I will reopen it. And today, it has more than two million followers.

What is next for the students? The demand for monarchical reform will need a push from political parties if it is to find traction; they must take it for a debate in parliament. In this role, they could act as a buffer for the students in deflecting the pressure from the lèse-majesté law and the Computer Crime Act. But the signs are not good. Political parties fear serious consequences if they support the students. Meanwhile, King Vajiralongkorn has remained silent. Should the protests continue and the legal mechanisms fail to tame the students, a violent crackdown may ensue. ⊗

Pavin Chachavalpongpun *is associate professor at Kyoto University's Centre for Southeast Asian Studies*

Another black day for Poland

Poland's re-election of right-wing President Andrzej Duda this summer was met with little international condemnation. The world should have screamed, writes **Katarzyna Kasia**

THE LEVEL OF anger on the streets of Poland has hit new heights since the country's top court ruled that the law allowing abortions to be carried out because of foetal defects was unconstitutional. Thousands of people organised mass demonstrations all over the country to fight for their reproductive rights and against the oppression of the right-wing government. The protesters were mainly young people, but in the streets I also saw taxi drivers, coal miners, football fans and farmers – all out supporting their girlfriends, wives and daughters.

Four years ago the "black protests" successfully stopped the authorities from tightening one of the most restrictive abortion laws in Europe – abortion was already permitted only in cases of grave foetal abnormalities, rape or incest, or if the pregnancy threatened the mother's life and health. But four years ago, Andrzej Duda hadn't been re-elected as president – a decision that has given extra legitimacy to the right-wing agenda.

For those who have been paying attention to Poland, the attack on women's reproductive rights was not unpredictable, and Duda's re-election was the watershed moment.

The campaign leading up to the presidential election of 2020 was done in a heightened state of chaos, with many issues that people could question in terms of legality. The date of the election was changed. Then, in the first part of the campaign – held in spring, before the decision to postpone voting – participants had to deal with the growing dangers of the pandemic. Some of them tried to be responsible, such as Civic Coalition candidate Małgorzata Kidawa-Błońska, who suspended her physical campaign in order to protect people from the virus.

But Duda, supported by the Law and Justice Party (PiS), minimised the dangers of the virus and conducted his campaign without any particular limitations. His strategy proved much more rewarding: Kidawa-Błońska lost almost all her supporters, and for the second part of the campaign the Civic Coalition replaced her with another liberal candidate, Warsaw mayor Rafał Trzaskowski. And thus Poland lost the only woman on the list of 10 participants in the race.

The entrance of Trzaskowski opened a new chapter in the campaign's dynamics and brought about a shift in the discourse used during meetings with voters and in the state media.

As the mayor of Warsaw, Trzaskowski – who was elected in 2018 in the first round of voting, beating the PiS candidate – presented himself as a progressive politician. He signed the Warsaw declaration on LGBTQ rights and announced a desire to follow World Health Organisation guidelines on integrating non-heteronormative sexual orientation into sex education in the city's schools.

Duda's language shifted to that of exclusion in an immediate response to Trzaskowski. The Civic Coalition candidate was depicted as an extreme danger to the sacred tradition of the Polish Catholic family, even though he never formally endorsed same-sex marriage, supporting civil partnership instead. Duda introduced the topic of LGBTQ people into the electoral battle, calling it an "ideology worse than communism".

But the list of accusations was longer: the "LGBT ideology" would "sexualise" Polish

RIGHT: Coat hangers on the street of a women's rights protest against the abortion law amendment in the city of Wrocław, Poland at the end of October

children, would ruin traditional family bonds, was opposed to the Catholic Church, and would destroy society.

During the PiS convention, Deputy Prime Minister Jarosław Kaczyński said the party considered "two communities fundamental, the family as one man, one woman and the children", and he opposed the West, where children can have "two mummies or two daddies" because homosexual couples have the right to adopt.

A strategy based on fear had already been successfully used by Kaczyński during previous election campaigns. In 2015, he claimed that Poland should not accept refugees because Middle East migrants might not only take Polish people's jobs away but also bring "parasites and protozoa".

In addition to whipping up anti-LGBTQ sentiment, Duda and other high-level PiS politicians used the campaign to set other priorities.

The Civic Coalition candidate was depicted as an extreme danger to the sacred tradition of the Polish Catholic family

High on the agenda was the continued reform of media laws – Duda and other PiS politicians have frequently admonished news outlets in Poland owned by foreign media companies for reporting stories critical of the ruling party.

And Duda made clear his support of a ban on abortions in most cases.

Until the last moment of the 2020 presidential election, everything was still possible and Polish society was arguably the most polarised it had ever been. Duda had the support of the ruling

ABOVE: A women's rights protest against the abortion law amendment in the city of Wrocław, Poland at the end of October

> The consequences of the ideological battle are a tragedy. The LGBTQ+ community has faced a wave of violence, both verbal and physical

→ party, the Catholic Church and state media. Trzaskowski was perceived as a progressive, pro-European candidate who could put an end to the nationalist domination of Polish politics.

In the end, the difference between the candidates was tiny: Duda won 51.2% of the vote, the slimmest presidential election victory since communism ended in Poland in 1989. More than 10 million voters supported Trzaskowski but in politics, as in the song, "the winner takes it all".

The consequences of the ideological battle are a tragedy. The LGBTQ+ community has faced a wave of violence, both verbal and physical, with many cities declaring themselves to be LGBTQ-free. People identifying as LGBTQ who live in these areas have faced a choice: emigrate, keep quiet or fight back. In some cities people protested against the anti-homosexual agenda. Queer activists placed signs at their borders, and attracted attention from the European Union. In July, the EU denied funding from its Structural and Cohesion funds to municipalities that declared themselves as "LGBT-free", because it viewed this as discriminatory and a violation of the EU Charter of Fundamental Rights. In response, the Polish minister of justice (and prosecutor-general) decided to support these municipalities with government funds.

And then there is the abortion ruling from the Constitutional Tribunal. At the time of writing it is yet to become formal law, but Duda has said that if approved by parliament he will sign it into law, imposing a near-total ban on abortions.

I fear that Duda will continue his work as a strong supporter of the ruling nationalist coalition, obediently signing laws that will limit the power of the judiciary, freedom in academia and media, and the rights of minorities and women.

The end of the year has brought Poland to a state of total chaos. The government is unable to fight the coronavirus crisis and, despite mass demonstrations, we're running out of ways to fight the new laws coming our way. With little independent media left, who will speak up for us? ⊗

Katarzyna Kasia is assistant professor at the Academy of Fine Arts, Warsaw

CREDIT: Zuza Gałczyńska/Unsplash

Tearing down the ivory tower

The Turkish president has closed an entire university in Istanbul by discreetly changing laws to allow him to shut down any educational body that scrutinises his rule. **Kaya Genç** fears for academia's future

49(04): 29/31 | DOI: 10.1177/0306422020981254

SINCE RISING TO power in 2002, Turkish president Recep Tayyip Erdogan has imprisoned scores of reporters and NGO leaders, closed magazines and television stations, banned democratic rallies and pride marches, annulled election results, shut down Twitter, YouTube and Wikipedia, and forced Netflix to remove a gay character from a Turkish rom-com. But never before has he seized control of a whole university, forcing all its eminent staff to resign, taking over their campus, libraries and other academic properties, and cutting bursaries of its Erasmus students to silence dissenting voices.

On 30 June, keeping his promise to "get rid of Turkey's opposition viruses" while fighting Covid-19, Erdogan cancelled the operating licence of Istanbul Şehir University, a prestigious university founded in 2009 that became an intersection point between Marxists, liberals and Islamists.

Şehir's founding principles were established through talks with the country's top intellectuals: Halil Berktay, an expert on the Armenian Genocide, the Harvard historian Cemal Kafadar, and two dozen others. Bilim ve Sanat Vakfı (Science and Arts) – a foundation co-established by Ahmet Davutoğlu, a professor of international relations who served as Turkey's penultimate prime minister before the position was abolished – administered Şehir for a decade, hiring seasoned scholars of Ottoman culture, politics and literature who held decolonising views and amassed large social media followings. But nowadays Davutoğlu's foundation is demonised, and its administrators are intimidated into silence.

Fatih Altuğ is a leading scholar of Turkish literature who ran Şehir's Comparative Literature Centre for more than a decade. He was 32 when he joined the college. Its promise to be a "democratic, pluralist institution not ruled by any political group" attracted him. The financial support of Murat Ülker, a leading industrialist and a founding member of Bilim ve Sanat Vakfı, was also encouraging. Before its closure, Şehir was the third highest salary-paying university in the country, after Koç and Sabancı, private colleges owned by two of Turkey's most prosperous tycoons.

Şehir's multiculturalist agenda prioritised public intellectualism, and the school's roster featured scholars who were outspoken about Kurdish rights. Altuğ describes their student base as "children of mostly conservative families who were very open to liberal or leftist forms of conservative thought". Students enrolled at Şehir were among the best in the country, chosen from among the 2,000 highest-scoring pupils in the country-wide university exam.

Şehir soon earned a "woke" reputation. When 1,128 intellectuals put out an anti-war petition in 2016 titled We Won't Be Subject to This Crime, six Şehir scholars were among the signatories. Erdogan called the signatories "traitors" to make sure they were prosecuted and imprisoned. A subsequent purge in Turkey's leading colleges paved the way to install his loyalists. But Şehir scholars were let off the hook after the college's administration refused to sack the signatories.

> *The government chose a curious moment to finally close Şehir: it did so during the Covid-19 crisis*

ABOVE: Students relaxing in the Şehir University campus, Istanbul, in 2009, the year it was founded. Today, the campus is overgrown and unoccupied

→ Şehir students, too, were fearless. One studied the representations of the Armenian genocide in the Kurdish novel. "It was a doubly dangerous theme," said Altuğ, "but we faced no problems." Another student wrote a thesis on Zaven Biberyan and Ahmet Hamdi Tanpınar, discussing an Armenian and a Turkish writer's representations of the Armenian genocide. "We heard nothing from the Higher Education Council. Perhaps they are not yet aware of the contents of these theses," Altuğ added.

But the scholar, now 43, is visibly shaken while recounting what happened next. After Erdogan fired Davutoğlu and abolished the prime ministerial post to build his one-man regime, Davutoğlu founded The Future Party and everything changed. By December last year, the former prime minister had become the most vocal critic of Erdogan's regime. Having amassed a wealth of insider information about Turkey's autocratic system, Davutoğlu quickly became a hate figure in the pro-government press. Soon, Şehir staff found themselves in the eye of an anti-Davutoğlu campaign.

"They called us 'untrustworthy liberals who hide themselves at Şehir'," recalled Altuğ. "We were called 'intellectuals who poison conservative kids'." One nationalist labelled Altuğ and his Şehir colleagues "orientalist zoologists who look at Turkish literature from a foreign perspective". In response, they changed their WhatsApp group's name to "Orientalist Zoologists".

The government chose a curious moment to finally close Şehir: it did so during the Covid-19 crisis. Its takedown of the college, swift and methodical, was a lesson in authoritarianism. News of Şehir's demise was drowned out among news about the pandemic, becoming one of the most under-reported stories of 2020 despite its enormous implications.

After appointing an administrative caretaker for the college, Erdogan published a decree in April which made it possible to close Şehir, as well as other private colleges, immediately instead of waiting for three years after a takeover as the law demanded. Altuğ had a 9am class on the day the takeover decree was announced. "Students were trying to get used to online education. Professors were trying to survive financially and not to reflect Şehir's difficulties to students. I talked with my class for 15 minutes about the situation. I felt I had to keep on doing my job properly despite our ordeals."

But that became impossible as Şehir stopped functioning. Food was no longer served in the school's cafeteria. Students on Erasmus

CREDIT: Image Professionals GmbH/Alamy

scholarships couldn't receive their money. Altuğ went unpaid for three consecutive months. Online education and Covid-19 made it easier to ignore the physical reality for a while, but after Ömer Çelik, vice-president of the ruling Justice and Development Party (AKP), announced that the school's operating licence was cancelled following an AKP central committee meeting, Altuğ realised he was "in stark denial of the situation". Closure was what the state wanted, and there was no escape from it.

In the summer, soon after the lockdowns lifted, he visited the school one last time to collect his belongings. "I had 20 boxes of books at my office," he said. "When I visited the campus in June, the security guards working at the college for a decade had been replaced by guards from a state college. After I entered the school premises, they accompanied me to my office. They waited there, taking notes about what I did inside, which boxes I took. This was one of the saddest moments of my life. This place, [which] once I considered home, I could now only enter by a guard shadowing me."

Under its caretaker, Şehir has turned into a ghost town. When Altuğ took a final walk on the campus, he saw that the grass was overgrown because gardeners had not mown it. In the past there had been great animal diversity on the campus with lots of cats, dogs and birds. Now there were just a few stray dogs. In the corridors there were photocopied papers scattered on the ground. "It was so sad to see it so deserted," he said.

The government also confiscated personal libraries donated to Şehir by families of the luminaries of Turkish social sciences: thousands of books by Taha Toros, Şerif Mardin, Kemal Karpat, Fuad Köprülü and Talât Sait Halman now belong to the caretakers.

In response to the closure, a group of students organised a protest as early as April. But when they came to the campus that month they were refused entry to Şehir. Şuhedanur Hacıalioğlu, a professional archer who plans to have an academic career in literature, was among those who protested at the university's gates.

"The conflict played out during my final year as an undergraduate," she told Index.

> *Hacıalioğlu and her fellow graduates tried to reach journalists to tell their stories, but intimidated reporters chose to ignore them*

"Once we understood its nature we began raising our voices on social media. As we did so we noticed how all other voices had sunk into silence." Hacıalioğlu and her fellow graduates tried to reach journalists to tell their stories, but intimidated reporters chose to ignore them. The platform she joined, Şehirhepimizin (Şehir Belongs to Us All), held meetings and planned marches and issued political statements. "Because I'm a literature graduate, I helped write the first statement. We went to the parliament and talked with MPs. We held our protest march. We just wanted to defend our school and raise our voices against injustice."

According to Altuğ, Turkey's academic community doesn't yet realise the significance of the decree which makes seizing universities easier. "It was created specifically for Şehir but it may help take over all private colleges in the country," he said. "The calamity has not yet been comprehended. Even if it is his own son's university, the president can find an economic or other excuse to take over a school overnight." He warns that if private colleges such as Koç, Sabancı and Bilgi rattle the government just one bit, they will face a similar end.

Today, Bilim ve Sanat Vakfı plans to take the case to the European Court of Human Rights, but with Erdogan's autocratic rule still in place, there seems little prospect that Şehir will be returned to its owners. "This can happen to any school from now on," Altuğ said. "And what we experienced will set the agenda and the tone for academic life in Turkey in the near future." ⊗

Kaya Genç *is contributing editor (Turkey) for Index. He is based in Istanbul*

Ganging up against the truth

El Salvador's president denies that his government is in bed with the country's biggest gang. **Chris Havler-Barrett** digs deeper

49(04): 32/34 | DOI: 10.1177/0306422020981267

PEOPLE IN EL Salvador are split over who truly controls the country. While the state is nominally in charge of order and governance, gangs - especially the infamous Mara Salvatrucha (MS-13) - have gained an unprecedented level of power and control over the population. This struggle between the military and MS-13 has culminated in the supremacy of one of the most notorious criminal organisations in the world. In response, both sides are trying to conceal the extent of this new paradigm - with freedom of expression increasingly under threat.

In September, online media outlet El Faro reported that the government of President Nayib Bukele had been negotiating with MS-13 to lower the murder rate and win members' support in mid-term elections in exchange for prison privileges. El Faro said it had obtained a cache of government documents to prove these claims. Bukele took to Twitter, denying the claims and attacking El Faro.

The incident has highlighted the issues now underlying politics in El Salvador. Dissidents are unable to speak out while there is a gang willing to kill anyone who protests against it and a government willing to cross the boundaries of the law to protect itself from criticism.

While the behaviour of Bukele, who has been in power since 2019, might seem relatively common among the aspiring autocrats of the Americas, there is a deeper problem illustrated by the revelations in El Faro. The government has lost control and has begun to restrict freedom of speech in an attempt to conceal this fact.

Miguel Angel Cruz Blanco is a professor of sociology at the University of El Salvador. He feels that explaining the evolution of MS-13 is essential to understanding the issues that the government is now desperate to conceal.

The genesis of the group, like much of the country, is rooted in the civil war that ran for more than a decade until the 1990s.

"There was a mutation of these gangs, from simply being groups of 'rebellious' youths, along with deported migrant children, into groups that were more profoundly criminal," he told Index. "This then afforded the gangs access into the Salvadorean establishment."

Politically, the first demonstration of gang power came in 2012 with the ceasefire agreement brokered by the government of Salvador Sánchez Cerén. The ceasefire, between MS-13 and bitter rivals Barrio 18, was aimed at reducing the astronomical murder rate in the country, but it overlooked all other crimes, allowing the gang to diversify activities while receiving lenience from the authorities.

The aggressively militarised *Mano Dura* (Iron Fist) anti-gang policies introduced by the conservative government of Antonio Saca and strengthened increasingly by his successors eventually led to conditions that collapsed the ceasefire. The subsequent response resulted in the Salvadoran murder rate becoming the highest in the world, at 105.4 per 100,000 during 2015.

This demonstration of power proved that MS-13 was above the rule of law. While the *Mano Duro* policies militarised the police, increasing violence and oppression against innocent Salvadorans, governments were negotiating under the table with the same gangs they targeted in the streets, achieving by crook what they could not by hook.

This forced communities to openly turn to the gangs for assistance, consolidating their popular support and allowing them to fill the vacuum left by the state. Cruz Blanco attributes the overall failure of the government to enforce control as a result of failing to understand this.

"Ever since the third Arena [Nationalist Republican Alliance] government, they have tried to use violence to fight greater violence, but they never bother to address the underlying issue, which is extreme inequality within El Salvador," he said.

Bukele's desire to strike back at media critics may be motivated by the trail of prosecutions and convictions of former leaders who have dealt with MS-13 in the past.

The architect of the 2012 truce, David Munguía Payés, was arrested this July for criminal activity relating to the establishment of the ceasefire. Most of the previous organisers were arrested in 2016. Of the seven post-war leaders of El Salvador, Antonio Saca is in prison, Mauricio Funes is in exile, Francisco Flores, architect of *Mano Duro*, died while on trial and Bukele is mired in corruption allegations.

What has effectively happened in El Salvador is a brutal form of regulatory capture, whereby MS-13 is able to operate with relative impunity across the region. "It is important to note", explained Cruz Blanco, "that during the early Arena administrations, the gangs had not reached anything near the levels of violence or power that they enjoy now."

Alma Ortensia Martínez Escobar works for the regional government in the west of El Salvador. "This goes even beyond freedom

BELOW: Members of the Mara 18 and MS-13 gangs at a prison in Izalco, El Salvador this September

Of the seven post-war leaders of El Salvador, Antonio Saca is in prison, Mauricio Funes is in exile, Francisco Flores, architect of Mano Duro, died while on trial and Bukele is mired in corruption allegations

CREDIT: Yuri Cortez/AFP/Getty Images

They have tried to use violence to fight greater violence, but they never bother to address the underlying issue, which is extreme inequality within El Salvador

→ of expression," she explained. "There are other fundamental rights that these gangs restrict, including freedom of movement. There are many young people who have been killed at the hands of these gangs."

This has created a state where there is no longer any clear delineation between right and wrong. While gang members subject victims to excruciating violence, abandonment of the people by successive governments and brutalisation by security forces mean that overall popular power and control are now on the side of MS-13 – rather than the government.

When asked if he believed that MS-13 held tangible political control of El Salvador, Cruz Blanco was direct in his assessment. "Yes. They do."

This loss of power shapes the desire of politicians in El Salvador (Bukele especially) to control the narrative. The illusion of control – that the government is in charge, and that the gangs understand their place – is an important one. Free reporting threatens this concept and has been increasingly targeted as the social situation has worsened in the country.

It is now very difficult to publicly criticise either side of the conflict. Bukele has demonstrated time and time again that he is willing to go beyond the law to prosecute his detractors, and MS-13 has demonstrated that it is happy to execute anyone it feels is threatening its dominance, as evidenced by the murders of several journalists documenting MS-13 activity over the course of the last decade.

Martínez is blunt when asked how openly people can express their feelings towards gangs. "For the people here, there is a certain fear when these groups are mentioned," she said. "It is necessary to face the reality that most Salvadorans have a family member involved in these criminal groups, so you cannot freely express your opinions for fear of your own security."

In the Reporters Without Borders (RSF) Press Freedom Index, El Salvador dropped 15 places during the first year of the Grand Alliance for National Unity government, and while it has recovered slightly (it's currently at position 74 of 180 countries), the recent clampdowns and intense coronavirus reporting restrictions are likely to cause an even greater decline in 2021.

Press freedom is eroding under the current administration and political freedom of speech in general is increasingly difficult. Emmanuel Colombié, RSF Latin America chief, expressed concern at the attitudes of the Salvadoran government.

"President Bukele's repeated attacks and threats against journalists critical of his administration signal an extremely worrying shift towards authoritarianism," he said.

"The systematic denigration and attempts to create the image of a press that is the enemy of the people are not just dangerous and counterproductive, they also reinforce the entire society's mistrust of journalists, whose reporting is nonetheless vital in a country badly affected by violence and corruption."

Ultimately, it matters relatively little why politicians have sought to negotiate with MS-13. What matters more is that they have surrendered power to a group that will not willingly return it and, as a result, placed El Salvador into a sociopolitical limbo that has no obvious point of return. With the unrestricted brutality of MS-13 reprisals on one side and the abuse of law on the other, freedom of speech in El Salvador is becoming ever-more limited.

As for the challenges facing the country in 2021, as long as Bukele is in power, there is unlikely to be a significant change in circumstances for anyone attempting to hold two sides of a brutal conflict to account. ⊗

Chris Havler-Barrett *is a freelance journalist based in Mexico City, who reports across Latin America*

The greatest story never told...

For a journalist, little can compare with the feeling you get when you secure a brilliant scoop—a public interest story that will make the headlines, hold the rich and powerful to account and change an unjust world.

Yet that thrill can quickly turn to fear when a legal threat lands on your doormat, warning you to desist on pain of of expensive and time-consuming legal action.

It should not be that way.

Strategic lawsuits against public participation—or Slapps—are increasingly used to silence journalists and cover up inconvenient truths.

Do you think you could be facing a Slapp? Use our tool to find out.

www.indexoncensorship.org/stopslapps

#STOPSLAPPS

Mexico's deadliest state

Following the removal from power of a corrupt official, the "official narrative" is that it is a lot less dangerous to be a reporter in the state of Veracruz. But recent events paint a different picture, reports **Stephen Woodman**

JULIO VALDIVIA'S COLLEAGUE immediately recognised his blue motorbike. It was lying flat across the railway tracks leading out of Motzorongo, a remote town in the eastern Mexican state of Veracruz. The journalist, who asked not to be named due to safety concerns, parked his car at the side of the road. At first, he thought Valdivia had crashed. But as he moved closer, he realised his friend had not had an accident. The reporter's battered body and severed head lay on the tracks a few feet from his bike.

Every 4 January, Mexico marks National Journalist Day with newspaper columns reflecting on the country's freedom of expression crisis. But there are no easy solutions for media workers in Veracruz, the single most dangerous place for the press in the deadliest country for journalists in 2020.

"We are totally defenceless," Valdivia's friend told Index. "State police act as if we are enemies and offer zero information… Walking through this region, you feel the darkness."

Journalists have paid for their refusal to censor, and 25 reporters have been killed in Veracruz in the past decade

The media crisis in the state of about eight million inhabitants is a product of its strategic location in Mexico's ongoing crime war. Cartels have long smuggled drugs through the Port of Veracruz. In the past decade, they have also diversified into activities such as extortion, kidnapping and fuel theft from pipelines.

Valdivia worked for El Mundo newspaper, covering the border region between Veracruz and the adjacent state of Oaxaca. The area is a key battleground for criminal gangs, including the Jalisco New Generation Cartel (CJNG), a sprawling syndicate now considered the country's top security threat.

Despite the dangers he faced, El Mundo reduced Valdivia's salary earlier this year. At the time of his murder, the journalist was earning the equivalent of about $47 a week. The father of six was buried in a metal casket because his family could not afford a wooden coffin.

"Journalists have endured massive salary cuts," said Ana Laura Pérez, the president of the Veracruz State Commission for Attention to and Protection of Journalists (Ceapp). Those economic difficulties have become even more complicated with the pandemic.

Pérez said that financial pressure on journalists was another form of censorship, reducing interest in the profession. "Reporters need better working conditions because they are the eyes of society," Pérez said. "Independent journalism is a vital part of a democratic state."

Veracruz became synonymous with corruption during the term of state governor Javier Duarte. Elected in 2010, Duarte stole vast sums of federal money designated for social initiatives in the state.

The governor allied with the CJNG against the Zetas cartel, which had previously controlled the state's illicit economy. Violence soared as he directed state security forces to murder and disappear suspected Zetas.

To avoid scrutiny, the state government spent about $430 million on advertising contracts with media outlets. In return, the administration expected favourable coverage.

Journalists who refused to comply became targets. Article 19, the press freedom campaign group, documented 271 acts of aggression against the press in Veracruz between 2010 and 2016. These included physical attacks, direct threats, abductions and harassment. On one occasion, Duarte's own security guards jostled with a photojournalist at the official signing of an agreement to protect freedom of expression.

Lethal violence against the press also escalated under Duarte. During his term of office, Veracruz recorded at least 17 killings of journalists and three disappearances.

Duarte announced he was resigning to face criminal charges in 2016. Instead, he fled Veracruz in a helicopter. After six months on the run, he was arrested in Guatemala and extradited to Mexico. After agreeing to plead guilty, Duarte received a nine-year prison sentence for organised crime association and money laundering. The light punishment sparked national outrage and he may now face further charges related to the enforced disappearance of a police officer. Duarte's ex-wife and suspected co-conspirator Karime Macías is fighting an extradition case after fleeing to London.

The current governor of Veracruz, Cuitláhuac García, says the freedom-of-expression crisis that peaked under Duarte is now under control. But rights groups offer contradictory accounts.

"The problem continues because of the political culture [in Veracruz]," said Ceapp's Pérez. "Our public officials are very intolerant of criticism. We have recently seen officials threatening media workers. If the boss maintains a negative attitude with the press, their subordinates know they can also violate their rights."

Freedom-of-expression studies show public servants, rather than drug traffickers, are the main violators of press freedom in Mexico. →

BELOW: A picture of murdered journalist Julio Valdivia on his coffin during his wake in Tezonapa, Veracruz, September 2020

The government estimates authorities across the country punish fewer than 1% of crimes against the press

→ But in many states, including Veracruz, the line between political and criminal interests has blurred.

During the past decade of violence, self-censorship has become the norm in many regions. In Veracruz, coverage of corruption and cartel-related crimes has reduced. But in contrast to the adjacent state of Tamaulipas, where investigative journalists have fallen silent, some reporters in Veracruz continue to cover political scandals and cartel activity.

"A small sector of the press held firm in its decision to report on these incidents," said the Inter-American Commission on Human Rights in a report on freedom of expression.

Journalists have paid for their refusal to censor, and 25 reporters have been killed in Veracruz in the past decade, according to Article 19. That figure accounts for nearly 30% of the total across the country.

After an international outcry, national and state authorities both introduced schemes to provide support measures such as security cameras and armed protection for at-risk journalists in 2012.

But such measures do nothing to address the underlying impunity driving the crisis. The government estimates authorities across the country punish fewer than 1% of crimes against the press. In Veracruz, no single case of a murdered journalist has been resolved.

Fernanda De Luna desperately hopes that situation will change. Following the murder of her mother, the journalist María Elena Ferral, in March, authorities issued arrest warrants for 11 suspects. Police have since detained six people. But De Luna, who is also a reporter, remains sceptical about the government's commitment to defending freedom of expression in the region.

Ferral was a correspondent for a local newspaper, El Diario de Xalapa, and co-founded the digital outlet El Quinto Poder with her daughter. Days before her death, she published a final column on her website. In that article, Ferral described the murder of four aspiring politicians in northern Veracruz. She identified the members of a powerful political group as the key suspects in the killings. "In this new political landscape, the fight for power will be brutal," Ferral wrote. "Without a doubt, there will be more political crimes in this region."

Later that month, a masked gunman on a motorcycle shot the 49-year-old as she left a notary's office in the city of Papantla. She was rushed to hospital but died later that day.

De Luna notes her mother had suffered violence in the past. In 2005, she was shot in the leg after providing a taped interview to the police linking local mayor Basilio Picazo to the murder of a former municipal official. Seven years later, unknown assailants shot into her car and caused a crash with another vehicle.

In 2016, Ferral accused Picazo of threatening to abduct and kill her during his campaign for Veracruz state congress. Following the threat, Ceapp assigned Ferral a bodyguard. But the government withdrew that protection the following year.

De Luna believes the murder was linked to her final publication. "When I read that column… I told her to be careful," she said. "But she always wanted to defend people and expose politicians that exploited them."

Less than two months after her mother's murder, De Luna was travelling by car through rural Veracruz. Gunmen started shooting from another vehicle but retreated when her bodyguards returned fire.

De Luna said the experience would not deter her reporting, which had transformed into a vehicle for channelling grief.

"My mother's passion was journalism and I want to carry on because I don't want to see our joint project fail," she said. "I know the risks, but I need to keep working."

Stephen Woodman *is contributing editor (Mexico) based in Guadalajara*

Europe's new Orban

Until recently Slovenia was viewed as liberal. But the appointment of a new prime minister this year cut from the same cloth as Viktor Orban is a cause for concern, writes **Anuška Delić**

SINCE HE CAME back into power as part of a coalition earlier this year, life in Slovenia under prime minster Janez Janša has felt more like Viktor Orban's Hungary than a moderate EU country.

The Slovenian Democratic Party (SDS) – and especially Janša, its leader – has long been flirting with neighbouring strongman Orban. Today, businessmen with ties to Orban own media that back the SDS. Minister of the interior Aleš Hojs, who was installed in March, previously led Nova24TV.si, which is owned by Orban's friends. Along with sister television station Nova24TV, it is among the main sources of disinformation in Slovenia.

Both Hojs and Janša regularly exhibit their disdain for media and journalists in Twitter attacks. Like Donald Trump, Janša uses the platform almost as an official government channel. For example, he used it to announce the second wave of the pandemic one Sunday evening in October. In November, he tweeted in agreement with Trump's false claim that he had won re-election in the US presidential election.

Twitter is also where Janša called two female reporters of the public broadcaster "presstitutes". It is where the SDS and its sympathisers have routinely labelled Slovenian journalists "communists" and "liars".

Much like Orban, who started his career on the other side of the political spectrum, Janša was once a hopeful young communist. He diligently led a pilgrimage to Jajce, a town in Bosnia that has historical significance for anti-fascists. In the 1980s, he was a dissident journalist with the weekly Mladina, and it was whilst working there that he was imprisoned for exposing military secrets.

After more than 25 years at the helm of the SDS, Janša is one of the longest standing leaders of a political party in Slovenia. He seems to have lost all taste for media freedom, and for freedoms more generally. As prime minister, he presides over public officials and party sympathisers who routinely attack, smear and lie about journalists.

And, again like Orban, Janša's political campaigns have been based on xenophobia, Islamophobia and hate speech.

Mere months after gaining power, the SDS has employed everything at its disposal to disrupt public broadcaster Radiotelevizija Slovenija (RTV SLO) and national press agency STA, while denouncing almost all other independent media. In July, the government proposed changes to laws which would financially cripple publicly run media and advance the interests of outlets that churn out news favourable to the government.

The relationship between the party and its propaganda machines – Nova24TV and Demokracija amongst others – is quite transparent. When the SDS wants to advance an agenda, the outlets run campaigns that are shared by party members and supporters on social media.

When Harlem Désir, the Organization for Security and Co-operation in Europe's representative on media freedom, warned Janša's government against attacking RTV SLO (Janša has called reporters working there liars who are overpaid and who misinform the public about the pandemic), Demokracija hit back →

I have been under police protection before, I have been smeared before, but I have never experienced anything like this

ABOVE: Hungary's current leader Viktor Orban (right) and Slovenia's new leader Janez Janša together at the European People's Party Summit in 2011

→ saying Désir was abusing his position for ideological reasons.

This year, the SDS's disregard for international norms was highlighted in an official reply sent to the Council of Europe by the Slovenian permanent representative – who ultimately answers to foreign minister Anže Logar of the SDS – regarding warnings about declining media freedom in Slovenia, which were posted on its platform by several media watchdog organisations (including Index). The reply was full of disinformation about media and attacks on journalists.

But the attacks on journalists spread beyond social media. As highlighted on the Index map chronicling press attacks due to Covid-19, investigative journalist Blaž Zgaga was subject to death threats and a smear campaign after submitting a request for information to the government about its management of the coronavirus crisis. The attacks led to a wave of hate mail and threats, and Zgaga said: "I have been under police protection before, I have been smeared before, but I have never experienced anything like this."

The effort to control the narrative has been all-encompassing, and even the country's national statistics office has become a target. The government abruptly dismissed the recently named director for no specific reason – a first in the history of that office.

Slovenian journalists are fighting back. In August, RTV SLO published a statement by the editor-in-chief of its news programmes, denouncing the attacks on its journalists. In October, editors of 22 of the largest Slovenian media outlets signed a public statement vowing that they would not bow under pressure.

But it didn't make a big difference. On 5 November, violent anti-government protests erupted in the capital, and Hojs was quick to accuse the media of complicity.

Slovenia will hold the rotating EU presidency next year. Will Janša use it as an opportunity to team up with Poland and Hungary against the other member states when it comes to discussions on democracy and rule of law?

No one knows when, or even if, Janša and the SDS will see through the fog of fake news its friendly media outlets produce. We can only hope it will be soon. For six months the country has been struggling with an unprecedented social and health crisis, yet its key officials seem to have a lot of free time to tweet all kinds of abuse at journalists. ⊗

Anuška Delić is the founder of Oštro, a non-profit centre for investigative journalism in the Adriatic region

GOOD GUY GONE BAD

BENJAMIN LYNCH looks at Janša's move from liberal to hardline

IVAN JANŠA, BEST known as Janez Janša, was born in the town of Grosuplje in central Slovenia, then Yugoslavia, in 1958.

Janša became interested in politics and was heavily engaged in the League of Communists party as a young man, a far cry from the right-wing nationalist policies he pursues today.

He graduated from university in 1982 with a degree in defence studies, which would later serve him well as minister of defence during the war of independence.

The independence movement became more and more significant during the 1980s. Janša wrote extensively in the independent magazine Mladina and promoted freedom of speech. Notably, Janša pushed to publish minutes from a meeting of the Yugoslav Communist Party in which it discussed clamping down on the increasingly critical Mladina. The event pitted Janša and the magazine against the government, and he was eventually arrested in 1988 for "betraying military secrets".

His arrest and subsequent imprisonment caused an outcry and mass protests. Janša was arrested alongside three others and the trial has since become known as the Trial of the Four.

The focus on their fate helped speed up the process for a more democratic Slovenia (by becoming a multi-party democracy) and, upon his release after six months, Janša became editor-in-chief of opposition publication Demokracija, until May 1990.

Janša helped the Slovenian Democratic Union party (formerly the Social Democratic Party of Slovenia) orchestrate independence from Yugoslavia in 1991 after being elected to parliament the year before. In 1993, he became leader of the party and has held this post ever since.

Despite his early beginnings as an independence figure and political prisoner, Janša has since faced criticism for his attacks on the media. Since independence, Janša has been Slovenian prime minister three times. His first term (2004-08) ended in controversy with accusations of interference in press freedom. His second term ended in accusations of corruption. In the same year, 2013, he was eventually imprisoned for soliciting bribes but his conviction was annulled because of a lack of evidence, and he denies the accusations.

Janša recently congratulated US president Donald Trump for "winning" the recent election and accused the "mainstream media" of "facts denying".

Democracy versus the people

Mali has been gripped by huge protests following a recent coup. But people are not protesting for more democratic freedom — far from it, writes **Andy Morgan**

AFTER THE MALIAN army arrested President Ibrahim Boubacar Keita and seized power on 18 August, one of the country's leading rappers, Mylmo, released a song called Coup de Point d'Interrogation (The Question Mark Coup). Using imagery worthy of a smash-and-grab heist movie, he suggested that the country's political elite had colluded with the new junta, the National Committee for the Salvation of the People (CNSP), to ensure an eventual return to business as usual.

Mylmo's assessment was at odds with the majority opinion. The hundreds of thousands of Malian citizens who had taken to the streets in the preceding months to protest against the rampant corruption, ineptitude and venality of Keita's democratically elected government saw the army as the saviour of a nation that was, until 2011, regularly lauded as a model of peaceful, stable and open-minded African democracy.

The fact that Mylmo was able to upload his song without fear of a midnight visit by men in jackboots is an indication of the relatively healthy state of freedom of speech in Mali. True, his audacity was rewarded by a deluge of abuse on Facebook, including threats to smash up his home in the capital, Bamako, (never carried out) which forced him to lie low for a while. It's also true that the government's violent crackdown of mass protests in Bamako on 10 and 11 July resulted in 11 deaths and more than 140 injuries, as well as the closing down of the internet during the unrest. But overall, Mali's journalists, bloggers, TV and radio presenters and rappers (who play a crucial role in the country's media mix) have been allowed to document the growing opposition to Keita (known by the acronym "IBK") with relative freedom.

Mali's biggest question mark hangs not so much over freedom of speech but over democracy itself. The events of August elicited wildly divergent reactions at home and abroad. The international community cried foul, lamenting the curtailment of IBK's five-year democratic mandate. But in Independence Square in Bamako, the crowds were jubilant, honking horns and waving Malian flags.

It is widely believed that Keita's regime was one of the worst in Mali's 60-year history as an independent nation. Not only did it fail to solve any of the country's deep-seated problems, it made them worse. When Keita came to power in 2013, voted in by a population traumatised by the events of 2012 (a civil war and jihadist occupation in the north, a military coup in Bamako), Mali had regained control over most of its territory with massive help from the French army. Now, two-thirds of the country is no longer under government control.

The jihadist threat has spread out from the far north and taken hold of the centre of the country, stoking ethnic tensions between sedentary farmers and nomads. Violence is at an all-time high. The Armed Conflict Location & Event Data Project, an international conflict monitoring project, recorded 300 civilian deaths in the first three months of 2020, up 90% on the previous quarter.

The UN peace-keeping mission Minusma documented 119 extra-judicial killings committed by Malian security forces during the same period.

Strikes, underfunding and mismanagement have brought the country's education, health and judicial systems close to collapse. Conflict and climate change have pulverised the farming sector. People are hungry. And meanwhile corruption runs rampant at all levels of government, with popular ire focused on IBK's son Karim Keita, who is accused of embezzling huge sums when he was in charge of the National Assembly's Defence Committee.

But it's France and the international community's insistence on applying democratic norms at all costs that angers many Malians. "In a country where there's no security, no justice, no schools, how can democracy function?" asked Choguel Maiga, former trade minister and one of the leaders of the M5-RFP protest movement, in an interview with Index.

> *When the people rise up to say they can stand it no longer, then the so-called international community form a bloc to suffocate the revolution*

BELOW: Protesters demanding President Keita's resignation in the capital Bamako, Mali, June 2020

CREDIT: Baba Ahmed/AP/Shutterstock

Every young Malian with a gun is a man – a brother, a son, a husband, a father

→ "People are dying in their thousands. The fight against terrorism exists in word only. And when the people rise up to say they can stand it no longer, then the so-called international community form a bloc to suffocate the revolution. Everybody bore witness to how the National Assembly elections [of March/April 2020] were rigged. All the Western ambassadors saw it. So in truth, it's not democracy. It's hypocrisy."

Malians have long suspected France of interfering in multi-party democracy to ensure that the candidate most favourable to its interests always wins. And it's clear that France's interests and those of the Malian people do not coincide. Where the latter crave security, food, jobs, education, health and non-corrupt governance, the former focuses doggedly on the fight against terrorism, stemming migration and the rigid application of democratic norms.

No wonder events and attitudes in Mali so often seem to come as a total surprise to foreign powers and observers. It's estimated that it costs France about $1.2 million for every "terrorist" killed by French special forces. And yet many of the people those special forces are supposed to be protecting feel nostalgic for the security that the armed jihadist groups imposed when they occupied the northern two-thirds of the country in 2012.

"Back then, security was guaranteed and justice assured," said Sane Chirfi, a teacher, writer and former head of the government tourism agency in Timbuktu.

"We saw armed men stealing cars and motorbikes at gunpoint and every time it happened, the so-called 'jihadists' intervened to return them to their owners. We saw cases of violence against women whose perpetrators were subsequently whipped. Then after the end of the occupation, insecurity became the norm – theft, rape, mugging, car-stealing on a daily basis."

Seckou Toure, a musician, agrees.

"It was better then. You could leave your motorbike out in the street and nobody would touch it. All the jihadists wanted was sharia. Now things are bad between us. It's just pure bandit-ism. That's the difference."

These testimonies, and dozens more I've heard from other northerners, beg this question: how is it possible to organise free and fair elections in territory where there's no security and no state control? Toure confirms that only the main towns in the Timbuktu region – Timbuktu, Niafunké, Diré, Goundam – are secured by the army and police. And the only safe means of travel through the region is by boat or pirogue up the Niger river. And yet in March and April this year, the government held National Assembly elections that were deemed to have 'proceeded well' according to a report by the Malian pool of citizen electoral observers POCIM. Local people know this to be a lie.

In March, Soumaila Cissé, the head of the main opposition party in the National Assembly, the URD, was kidnapped by an al-Qaeda-affiliated jihadi group whilst on the campaign trail near Niafunké. He was released only on 12 October. Imagine Joe Biden being kidnapped but the US presidential election still going ahead in a "free and fair" manner.

Perhaps, sadly, that doesn't sound as far-fetched as it should, but the point is that real democracy in Mali appears impossible at the moment. Not only because of the insecurity, the corruption and the lack of democratic "awareness" amongst much of Mali's illiterate population but because many have simply lost faith in democracy itself.

"For years and years, Mali was held up as a fine example of democracy while it wasn't true at all," said a Malian UN employee who wished to remain anonymous. "I don't think the international community paid much attention. They didn't give a damn. Even though elections were held, and observers were here, there was so much stuff happening – stuff you couldn't miss. And gradually people lost faith in elections. When you mention elections now, it's 'Oh, no, it's never going to be fair, so why bother voting for someone?"

After Cissé was freed, he gave an interview to Le Monde in which he was asked what

FAR FROM INDEPENDENT

It's been 60 years since Mali gained independence from France. But as BENJAMIN LYNCH highlights looking at its recent history, independence hasn't always meant freedom

1960
The French colony gains independence as part of the Mali coalition. When fellow coalition members Senegal and Sudan withdraw, the Republic of Mali comes into existence. The new republic – which celebrates its independence every September – is led by Mobido Keïta.

1960-68
Keïta declares a socialist state, which sees his opponents routinely imprisoned. By 1968, Keïta's grip on power slips and a military coup allows Moussa Traoré to seize power. Keïta is arrested and imprisoned and Traoré enforces a police state over the coming years.

1975
The Democratic Union of the Malian People is formed by Traoré in 1975, moving Mali to a one-party state. Traoré declares himself general secretary and he and his party win the next two presidential and four national assembly elections with 100% of the vote.

1980
There is a clampdown on student and teacher protesters and students die in detention. Public memorials take place in July but are dispersed. Up to 40 teachers are taken into custody.
But during this decade Traoré does allow some new media to start up, as Index documented at the time.

1990
Exiled opposition leader Bassirou Diarra is arrested and released. Unrest in Mali grows due to austerity programmes.

1991
Protests continue and a peace agreement is briefly reached. Still, protests are met strongly by police. In March, an estimated 148 civilians are killed in what becomes known as the March Revolution.
Soldiers increasingly refuse to fire at civilians. By the end of the month, after fierce rioting, the military arrest Traoré. Steps towards a multi-party democracy begin to take place and a "permissive media environment" is allowed.

1992
Alpha Oumar Konaré is elected president.

2002
The new constitution proposes a two-term limit on the presidency and Konaré leaves in 2002. Amadou Toumani Touré becomes president.

2007
Five journalists are convicted on charges of insulting Touré.

2012
The Mali War breaks out. Touré is ousted in a coup d'etat fought by several insurgent groups who seize control of areas of the country.

2013
Elections are held and president Ibrahim Boubacar Keïta takes charge. His control of Mali results in restricting press freedom.

2020
Street protests against Keïta begin, and in August there is another coup.

---

lessons he had learned from his experience. "What I'll remember is that in front of us are men," he answered, referring to his Islamist captors. "Today, everybody's saying that we have to smash terrorism in the face, but we need to extract ourselves from that dogma."

That's true. Every young Malian with a gun is a man – a brother, a son, a husband, a father – who has chosen this path because he saw no other viable way to survive the anarchy in northern Mali.

Toure, the musician, said: "There's no work, no money. That's what pushes people into crime. If there was work and everyone was earning a little money, none of that would exist."

The West's often knee-jerk aversion to politicised Islam is misplaced. The reason that imam Mahmoud Dicko, former head of the High Islamic Council and de-facto political leader of M5-RFP, is the most popular man in Mali right now is because he's seen to be above the mire of Malian politics. His decision to "return to the mosque" after the coup and leave the transition to the soldiers and career politicians only reinforced this opinion. Malians are desperate for leaders who can show they understand the needs of the common people.

The Malian people put democracy in the dock on 18 August. Now it's time to listen carefully to their testimony. ⊗

Andy Morgan is a writer and journalist who focuses on West Africa and the Sahara. He is author of Music, Culture and Conflict in Mali

"The state won't protect you"

The arrest of a leading author is just one example of how Robert Mugabe's death has not brought about the hoped-for improvements to rights in Zimbabwe, writes **Natasha Joseph**

49(04): 46/48 | DOI: 10.1177/0306422020981274

IT SHOULD HAVE been the best week of Tsitsi Dangarembga's life. At the age of 61, the author, filmmaker and activist who exploded onto the literary scene in 1988 with her debut novel Nervous Conditions had just learned that she'd made the Booker Prize longlist. Her third novel, This Mournable Body, wasn't just Booker-worthy: it was gaining critical and commercial acclaim around the world.

Instead, just three days after the longlist was released, Dangarembga was among scores of people arrested in Zimbabwe's capital, Harare, during anti-government protests. By September, This Mournable Body was on the Booker shortlist and its author's trial (for inciting violence and breaching health regulations related to Covid-19) had been repeatedly delayed.

To those watching from outside the southern African nation, it beggared belief: in many countries Dangarembga would be hailed by her own government as an icon, her global success a reason to celebrate. But Zimbabwe – whose citizens desperately hoped the military coup that finally deposed Robert Mugabe as president in 2017 would usher in wholesale political, social and economic change – isn't "many countries". Under Emmerson Mnangagwa, the current president, the iron fist that defined Mugabe's 30-year stranglehold on power shows no signs of softening.

Dangarembga told The Guardian in August that she was "afraid"; several opposition politicians and activists had been abducted in the run-up to the protest at which she was arrested. Journalist Hopewell Chin'ono was also languishing in Zimbabwe's notorious Chikurubi maximum security prison charged with "incitement to participate in public violence". He recorded police entering his home on 20 July, sharing the video on a Facebook livestream. His lawyer later said Chin'ono had been "abducted" without a warrant. And the "evidence" showing that he incited others to participate in public violence? He had highlighted alleged Covid-19 procurement fraud within the country's health ministry.

On 3 November, Chin'ono was rearrested at his Harare home. Legal insiders suggested the arrest was prompted by a tweet in late October in which he claimed that Zimbabwe's chief justice had intervened to initially deny him bail after his detention. One of the conditions of his bail was an effective ban on his use of social media for anything that might be read as critical of the ruling party.

If none of this makes sense to you, you're not alone. As Tony Reeler, a senior researcher at Zimbabwe's Research and Advocacy Unit, told Index: "Zimbabwe has been surreal since 2000."

Reeler, who was formerly the unit's director, has watched ruling party Zanu-PF lurch from one crisis to the next – and become ever more brutal – for decades. His background in law and psychology led him through academia and eventually into civil society. That is not an easy space in Zimbabwe as its various regimes, both pre and post-independence from Britain in 1980, have never trusted dissenting voices.

This is one of the most sophisticated thug governments in the world. They use extremely complex mechanisms of torture to manage dissent

In 2000, the Movement for Democratic Change emerged as a new opposition party to challenge Zanu-PF's dominance. The state responded with violence and suppression. It was a close-run affair but Zanu-PF retained power in what many still consider a stolen election. Since then, polls have been marred by violence and controversies, and allegations of vote-rigging have bedevilled every election, including the 2018 poll that brought Mnangagwa to power.

The surreality that Reeler refers to plays out in daily life. Zimbabwe's economy has plumbed new depths since Mnangagwa took over; Covid-19 has delivered even more financial misery for ordinary Zimbabweans, hitting the country's powerful, even vibrant, informal economy hard. And yet, Reeler said, on the streets of cities like Harare "there's a veneer of functioning". Much of that veneer is made possible by remittances from Zimbabweans who have left home in search of better prospects. "Remittances are a mask," Reeler said. "And it's slipping."

The situation is especially dire in the rural areas that represent Zimbabwe's real electoral battlefields. "That's where the voters are, and it's the heartland of deep poverty," Reeler said.

Covid-19, of course, has exacerbated existing crises as well as bringing new ones: "It's slow. It's hard. People are hungry. People are dying."

And people are increasingly fighting back. But many are doing so quietly, behind the scenes, for fear of violent repercussions. A report by research network Afrobarometer ahead of the 2018 polls found that 76% of respondents were always careful about what they said in public, evidence of how chilling government crackdowns on free expression have been. Many activists who Index contacted said they preferred not to engage with the media; most won't respond to emails because they fear they are under government surveillance and mistrust electronic communication. Still, there is a sense that people's patience has run out. What, many outside the country might ask, has taken them so long?

Reeler said: "Many Zimbabweans still have memories of the civil war in the 1970s. There were so many deaths. So many people grew up restricted. People want peaceful change through the ballot – but that's a naive hope.

"Passivity masks an enormous amount that's going on. Zimbabweans look after each other, that's how we've hung on."

ABOVE: Journalist Hopewell Chin'ono, who was arrested in July (and again in November), arrives at court in Harare, Zimbabwe in August 2020

CREDIT: Philimon Bulawayo/Reuters

People are increasingly fighting back. But many are doing so quietly, behind the scenes, for fear of violent repercussions

→ Covid-19 is making it increasingly tough for people to support each other as they have always done. Remittances from the diaspora have fallen drastically and, with them, the livelihoods that people have been able to generate for themselves.

The government seems unable and unwilling to respond in a way that might build bridges. Instead, it is cracking down on any acts or statements it perceives as dissent. Legislation is one arrow in its quiver. The Committee for the Protection of Journalists' Africa programme coordinator Angela Quintal points to two proposed laws as being particularly worrying: the Cyber and Data Protection and Patriotic bills. The latter would bar Zimbabweans from meeting foreign government representatives without government permission.

Quintal told Index that the mooted cyber law was too broad. She said: "As we have seen with the use of cybercrime laws elsewhere, it can be abused by the government hellbent on staying in power and violating the civil liberties of citizens.

"The opposition to the Zimbabwean government is playing out on social media and that's where the government is taking the fight. Zimbabweans are very active on social media, even though internet penetration is low, so it is obviously of concern to the government. Mnangagwa himself has complained about social media, so none of what we are seeing in Zimbabwe as the government tries to counter what it perceives as subversion should come as a surprise."

Reeler concurs. The government's moves to quash any opposition are precisely what you'd expect given that "Zanu-PF has no political trust, and no support base".

"All they have left is coercion. They know that the moment they take their foot off our necks…" Reeler trailed off. His organisation has offered support and assistance to many activists who've borne the brunt of that jack-booted foot in recent years. The ruling party has practised its cruel craft exceptionally well for decades.

"This is one of the most sophisticated thug governments in the world. They use extremely complex mechanisms of torture to manage dissent. [For instance] at the local level there are youth militias that mobilise when anyone speaks up – and then the soldiers move in. The longevity of this system has created a realistic, appreciable fear of elections and of participating in political life."

Women are particularly vulnerable. In May, three women members of the MDC were allegedly abducted from police custody, tortured and sexually assaulted. They had been arrested while attending a protest and charged with contravening Covid-19 lockdown rules. One of the three, MP Joana Mamombe, was photographed weeping in her hospital bed as she detailed the ordeal. The trio now face more criminal charges: the justice minister says they faked their abduction and lied about being tortured. Mamombe was later rearrested for allegedly violating her bail conditions after she failed to appear in court. At the time, she was in hospital on her psychiatrist's instructions.

Reeler told Index that attacks on women, especially those involving sexual violence, served as "a warning to women", reinforcing Zanu-PF's patriarchal politics.

"It's a way of saying 'Why be a politician? The state won't protect you'."

Yet Reeler remains optimistic that a change is coming. It will, he believes, be driven by Zimbabwe's youth. As is the case across sub-Saharan Africa, the country has an extremely young population. "The youth are getting feisty. They will crush Zanu-PF one day." ⊗

Natasha Joseph *is a freelance editor and journalist based in South Africa*

Dying for the mother tongue

People in Inner Mongolia have killed themselves as a political protest against the Chinese government. **Uradyn E Bulag** looks into why

IN THE COURSE of less than three weeks, between late August and the middle of September, an unprecedented protest erupted in Inner Mongolia, an autonomous region in north China. The Mongols were protesting against the introduction of so-called "nationally compiled" Chinese language textbooks in three core subjects (language and literature, politics and history) in Mongolian primary and middle schools. Starting this year, by 2022 all three subjects will be taught in Mandarin Chinese. If fully implemented, it would amount to eliminating the core of the Mongolian language teaching curriculum within the education system.

These changes were presented as a benefit to the Mongols, who were said to be in dire need of a good command of Mandarin Chinese so as to find employment in a market dominated by the language. The keyword used in the official instruction was for Mongols to "*zouchuqu*" – go out, that is, into the Chinese world.

Compared with Xinjiang and Tibet, where a similar programme has been introduced recently, the Inner Mongolia programme appears less hard-hitting. The Mongolian language is still to be taught, not as a separate course but combined with Mandarin Chinese under a singular module, "language and literature". Why, then, did the Mongols react so vehemently to this programme, which was ostensibly offered as a gift from the Chinese government? Why did Mongol students storm out of classrooms and gated campuses to the cheers of anxious parents waiting outside as police in full riot gear waded in to capture students and send them back to schools? And why did at least eight Mongols kill themselves in protest?

Those who took their own lives included a government official, a primary school principal, teachers, parents and a student.

Their deaths hardened the resolve of the government. By the middle of September it had sacked a number of Mongol officials and hunted down thousands of protesting parents whose photos had been circulated to the public in an effort to help catch them.

Mongols in Inner Mongolia are known as a cheerful people, often referred to as *uujuu taivan* – broad-hearted and tranquil. Suicide is extremely rare (the only cases on this scale happened during the Cultural Revolution when many Mongols were forced to confess alleged nationalist crimes and name names). They can also be tough-minded, not easily broken by hardship or pressure. Killing themselves for their language is thus an unprecedented development after decades of relative peace in Inner Mongolia.

What is so special about the Mongolian language that is worth dying for? After all, the majority of the Mongols already send their children to schools where Mandarin is the primary language. Perhaps it's because the government, without provocation and without warning, moved to deprive them of the last vestige of the Mongolian identity. *Eh hel* – mother tongue →

Perhaps it's because the government, without provocation and without warning, moved to deprive them of the last vestige of the Mongolian identity

Faced with this stark choice, most people have accepted the state's edict, at least for the moment

→ – was central to their protest. Promoted by Unesco, a mother tongue is a basic human right that no one should be deprived of. International Mother Tongue Day is now celebrated throughout the world, including China.

"Mother tongue" in China has actually become a rallying cry to celebrate linguistic diversity, opposing the dictatorship of the official Mandarin Chinese (*Putonghua*) which the government is promoting as the lingua franca to be spoken by each and every one of the 1.4 billion people of 56 distinct nationalities, many with their own language systems. In fact, many ethnic Chinese speak various Sinitic languages such as Cantonese (*Yueyu*), Shanghainese (*Huyu*) and Hokkien (*Minnanyu*), which are mutually unintelligible. Cantonese speakers in Guangdong province and now Hong Kong, Shanghainese, and Hokkien speakers in Fujian province are also bitter about being prohibited from being taught in their mother tongues.

But the Chinese rationale for banning minority languages is different from banning non-Mandarin languages within the Chinese language family in schools. Unlike Cantonese, Shangainese or Hokkien people, who are among the most economically advanced and prosperous, minorities including the Mongols are always considered backward, despite the fact that the Mongolian educational level is very high. Cultural prejudice dies hard. Today, minority autonomy and minority cultural rights are seen as obstacles to achieving a prosperous nation for all – the central promise of the Xi Jinping regime to minorities.

In this light, minority identity is under attack. It is no longer a collective right enshrined in the constitution or promised by party leaders. Instead, it has become an obstacle to the minorities concerned, now clashing with a newly imagined shared linguistic community. How to articulate the need for maintaining one's cultural identity including the mother tongue requires considerable political skill and eloquence in China today.

Leaked video clips show Mongols debating with Chinese officials sent to persuade them to send their children back to school. The debates were conducted in Mandarin, with the Mongols speaking impeccable Mandarin – often better than the Chinese officials. Mongols repeatedly emphasise that they have never shunned learning it, even in Mongolian schools. Graduates from Mongolian schools are highly successful, with many admitted to China's flagship universities such as Tsinghua. In other words, Mongol students from Mongolian schools excel because they have been educated bilingually. Mongols insist that, far from rejecting Mandarin Chinese, their only request is that primary school children be taught Mongolian, their mother tongue, first.

The Mongols' request was often persuasive to local officials. However, higher authorities continued to pressure parents to end their protests and send their children back to school. Mongols were exhorted to fulfil their political duty as a "model minority nationality" to implement this programme. Being a model minority now requires downplaying one's distinct cultural identity and accepting the undermining of education in one's mother tongue. Mongol cadres and teachers, the paragons of this model nationality, as party and state employees, have been given a choice: either fulfil their new political duty or face severe punishment for being nationalists, secessionists or troublemakers. Faced with this stark choice, most people have accepted the state's edict, at least for the moment, but some chose what they saw as the only alternative: the sacrifice of their own lives.

Many fear what might come next. They look at what has happened in Xinjiang and Tibet, where initial small infringements on the freedom to practise cultural traditions have

CREDIT: Byambasuren Byamba-Ochir/AFP/Getty

ABOVE: Protesters in the Mongolian capital of Ulaanbaatar demonstrating against replacing the Mongolian language with Mandarin Chinese in schools in neighbouring Inner Mongolia

led to full-scale attacks on their people. If they give away their language, what else will they be asked to sacrifice?

For now, the dust seems to have settled, and one can hear Mongol students reciting Mandarin Chinese texts in class. This is perhaps the new normal. Mongols may have lost their struggle but they have at least earned some recognition for their peaceful protest. Above all, they have contributed to the global struggle for the most basic human dignity: the right to speak one's own language. The Mongols who sacrificed their lives will be remembered as most likely the world's first martyrs for the mother tongue. ⊗

Uradyn E Bulag is reader in social anthropology at Cambridge University. His research often focuses on China and Inner Asia

GLOBAL VIEW

Hey, big brother – we're watching you

Ruth Smeeth remembers all those whose governments took away their freedoms long before Covid-19 did, and why we will fight extra hard for them

THE WORLD WAS shocked when 47-year-old French teacher Samuel Paty was brutally murdered this October in a Parisian suburb, simply for teaching his students about the basic human right of free speech. A right that is protected by both the French constitution and the European Human Rights Act. A right that we cherish and celebrate. His "crime" was to show his students the cartoons published by Charlie Hebdo which mock all religions, including Islam.

Paty embodied the best of us. As a public servant, he refused to be cowed and continued to teach the universal values of free speech and free expression. His assassination is a reminder of the fragility of our rights and how we must not only cherish them but fight for them.

In the face of a global pandemic, with populist leaders around the world attempting to impose their will and a US president seeking to undermine his own democracy, fighting for our rights has never been more important.

This has been a difficult year. Covid-19 – a virus none of us had heard of 12 months ago – has touched all our lives. We've lost friends and loved ones. We have missed those experiences which shape a year – birthdays, holidays and anniversaries. And we've missed those moments when intimacy is so important. No hugs of comfort when someone is grieving, no touch of reassurance when someone is struggling and no joyous embraces in celebration. It's affected all of us in untold ways.

But whilst most of us have been muddling through as best we can, the reality for too many people around the world is that the pandemic has barely changed their day-to-day experiences and is just one more problem for them to deal with. People such as Iranian writer and human rights defender Golrokh Ebrahimi Iraee, who is currently in one of the country's most dangerous prisons. Or Ahmet Altan, who as of mid-November had been detained in Turkey for 1,500 days. Or Algerian journalist Khaled Drareni, who was imprisoned in March after he reported on the protest movement that swept his country in 2019.

These three defenders of free speech represent millions of people who are currently incarcerated because of the political battles they have fought, the stories they have exposed, or who they are, like the millions of Uighurs in Xinjiang province, China. For all of them, Covid-19 hasn't taken the touch of their loved ones away – their governments had already done that.

This is why Index exists – to expose repressive regimes, to tell the world what is happening on our watch and to put a face to each story. Index highlights the people behind the headlines and makes sure that no one can use the excuse of ignorance for why more hasn't been done to help and protect them. Never has our voice been needed more.

This year has seen daily attacks on our free speech around the globe, from the introduction

For all of them, Covid-19 hasn't taken the touch of their loved ones away – their governments had already done that

GLOBAL VIEW

of the National Security Law in Hong Kong, through fraudulent elections in Belarus, to emergency legislation around the world being used as a front to restrict the free press.

And those are just the actions of repressive regimes. We've also seen the intensification of a "culture war" by some in the UK and the USA as they seek to stifle debate and instigate a form of self-censorship. Our roles at Index are to expose formal censorship and attacks on free expression by nation states, and to campaign to ensure that those people who have the right to free speech are able to use it.

In 2021 we will, of course, keep fighting the good fight in every one of these areas and more. The year also marks the 50th anniversary of the founding of Writers and Scholars International, our charitable organisation, so we will be reflecting on where Index should focus and what our role should be as we plan for the next 50 years.

But some decisions have already been made. We will be expanding our work on China and the Chinese Communist Party, exposing not just what's happening to the Uighurs but also events in Inner Mongolia and, indeed, further afield. We'll ask one of the most pressing questions of our time: how is the Chinese government using its economic might to censor cultural activities outside its borders?

We will also be building on our education programme, launching a new debate series exploring issues such as the role of free speech in protest movements and who is being cancelled and why.

After the pain and challenges of 2020, Index will be relaunching in 2021 to make sure we are fighting-fit for the battles ahead, because if this year is anything to go by we have lots of work ahead of us.

And with that, please do keep safe. ⊗

Ruth Smeeth is CEO at Index

ABOVE: A rally in Paris following the murder of the teacher Samuel Paty in October

MAIN: A Uighur man prays in the courtyard of a mosque in Xinjiang back in 2005

IN FOCUS

56   **LONG MARCH TOWARDS CULTURAL GENOCIDE** NICK HOLDSTOCK
A look at how the dire situation for Uighurs in China reached this point

61   **HOW TO CHALLENGE CHINA** TOM TUGENDHAT, RUSHAN ABBAS, ANNE-MARIE BRADY, LOKMAN TSUI
Experts tell us how we can all play a part in standing up to a silencing power

64   **ABUSE NOT PART OF JOURNALIST'S DAY JOB** FRÉDERIKE GEERDINK
In the Netherlands, a journalist won a landmark case against her online abusers

66   **TWO FACES OF ON LIBERTY** JOHN GRAY
Censorship is creeping into modern liberal institutions. Is philopsher John Stuart Mill at fault?

70   **OUT WITH THE OLD?** ROBERT SPEEL
Are Donald Trump's antics really out of the ordinary? This look at US history challenges such assumptions

73   **THE SUDANESE REVOLUTION WILL BE ILLUSTRATED** ABRAHAM T ZERE
A profile of Khalid Albaih, the artist starting much-needed but controversial conversations

76   **SOCIAL MEDIA PLATFORMS HAVE A MORAL DUTY TO BAN MISINFORMATION ABOUT VACCINES** JONATHAN KENNEDY, JULIE LEASK
Should we censor vaccine misinformation to protect vulnerable people? These experts debate the issue

Long march towards cultural genocide

With the persecution of China's Uighurs showing no sign of abating, **Nick Holdstock** looks at how the region reached this point

WHEN I USED to give talks about Xinjiang, I invariably began with images of crowded bazaars, Arabic writing, Friday crowds at mosques. I would present my audiences with photos of Uighur women wearing headscarves, rows of naan bread, small houses painted white and blue. They would see mounds of dried fruit, Uighur men wearing square skullcaps, smoke rising from kebab stalls. The aim of these somewhat clichéd tourist snapshots was to show my audiences how different this western region was from the China they knew or imagined. It seemed the best place to begin.

But since 2017 one fact has overwhelmed all other considerations when talking about the region. People who had previously never heard of Xinjiang now know that it is a place where more than a million people, most of them Uighurs, have been detained and subjected to intimidation, violence and indoctrination. None of these people has been charged with a crime. They were selected because they said or did something that the authorities regarded as a sign of "religious extremism" – a concept defined so loosely by them that simply having a beard, speaking one's native language, downloading the wrong app on a phone or being in contact with relatives in another country are regarded as suspicious.

Officially, the camps are "re-education centres" which people have voluntarily entered to acquire vocational skills and learn Mandarin (which is a second language for Uighurs). According to the authorities, the camps are thus fighting both poverty and extremism.

Outside the camps, the state seeks to regulate every aspect of daily life in Xinjiang. People are subject to intense digital and human surveillance, even in their homes, where government officials interrogate residents about their patriotic and religious beliefs. A wrong answer can get you sent to the camps. There have been campaigns discouraging the use of veils and head coverings for Uighur women in favour of "modern" clothing and make-up. Some common children's names have been banned for being too Islamic. Thousands of mosques have been destroyed or damaged; according to a recent report by the Australian Strategic Policy Institute think-tank, there are now fewer than at any time since the Cultural Revolution.

Those not sent to the camps are still at risk of ending up in a forced labour programme: factories suspected of using forced labour are part of the supply chains of many leading tech and textile corporations. Between 2017 and 2019, about 80,000 Uighurs were transferred to factories outside Xinjiang.

The collective impact of these and other policies has been to traumatise and intimidate the Uighur population. Yet despite widespread international condemnation, there's little chance of a policy change. In a recent speech, China's leader Xi Jinping declared that the Communist Party's strategy was "completely correct" and that the "the sense of gain, happiness and

OPPOSITE: School children in front of the Id Kah Mosque in Kashgar, Xinjiang in April 2019

CREDIT: Geovien So/Getty

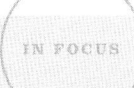

security among the people of all ethnic groups has continued to increase".

Constructing and maintaining the camps has required huge bureaucratic effort and financial investment, and exposed China to considerable criticism. So what has prompted the state to go to such lengths?

The Communist Party's core justification has been that tackling religious extremism will →

The decision to target an entire ethnic group suggests that the Chinese government views Uighurs as inherently predisposed towards 'religious extremism'

→ prevent terrorism. Since 2001 it has claimed to be at risk from Islamist terror groups with links to the Taliban, al-Qaeda and Isis, whose shared aim is to separate Xinjiang from China. During the early years of the "war on terror", China was able to get its claims endorsed by the US government and the plethora of security "experts" that emerged after 9/11, despite a lack of evidence that any such organised threat existed.

Over the past two decades, the Chinese government has used this narrative both to stifle dissent within Xinjiang and to explain the sporadic confrontations between Uighurs and the state. Some of these have been large protests, such as in the north-western town of Ghulja in 1997 and Urumqi, the regional capital, in 2009, but in most cases the incidents have been small-scale clashes between ordinary people and the army or police. In the overwhelming majority of these incidents there's been little credible evidence that either jihadist ideology or separatism has been the inspiration. Instead they appear to have been in reaction to state policies that have caused religious and economic discrimination, arbitrary arrests, forced disappearances and the marginalisation of the Uighur language and culture. Even the mildest criticism of these policies has been met with harsh penalties – in 2014, scholar Ilham Tohti was given a life sentence for suggesting that Xinjiang be granted more autonomy.

One of the factors which led to the decision to construct the camps was most likely the escalation in violence related to Xinjiang in

BELOW: Uighurs line the street for an official ceremony in 2008 to remember the 16 Chinese police officers killed in an alleged terrorist attack in Kashgar, Xinjiang

2013. In October that year, a car containing Uighurs crashed into a wall and exploded on the edge of Tiananmen Square in Beijing, killing five people. In March 2014, knife-wielding attackers killed 31 people in a railway station in Kunming, the capital city of the southern province of Yunnan. Later that year, two bombings in Urumqi, in Xinjiang, killed 45.

These were, by most definitions, terrorist acts, and probably any state would have responded by increasing security (though at this point Xinjiang was already a region with some of the heaviest security on the planet, with virtually omnipresent police and military). While these incidents alone might have been sufficient to elicit the same policy shift, the conjunction of several other factors made this more probable.

The first was the accession of Xi to power in late 2012. Within his first year of taking office, it was clear he was determined to suppress dissent in any form: lawyers, journalists, Christians, activists, bloggers and rivals within the party were all targeted. Xi also stressed the importance of "patriotic education" in building a national identity that transcends regional or ethnic identity, which – although already a cornerstone of Communist Party ideology – he has promoted particularly aggressively. Under his leadership, it's almost unthinkable that there would have been any easing of control in Xinjiang.

His appointment of Chen Quanguo as the region's top official in 2016 was an early signal that a severe response was to follow. During his time as party secretary in Tibet from 2001 until 2016, Chen introduced re-education facilities, though on a small scale, as well as networks of urban police stations that acted as checkpoints.

Then there is Xinjiang's location. Situated in China's far west, in the early years of the People's Republic of China, it was primarily important as a buffer region between China and the Soviet Union. But after the economic reforms of the 1980s, it became a vital part of the national economy, especially as a source of oil, gas and minerals. Xinjiang also plays a key role in the Belt and Road Initiative, China's bid to construct a new global infrastructure network by improving sea, road and rail transportation. Put simply, a lot of goods and resources will be passing through the region, and thus it needs to be perceived as a stable environment in order to encourage investment and workers from inner China to relocate to the region.

> *Even the mildest criticism of these policies has been met with harsh penalties – in 2014, scholar Ilham Tohti was given a life sentence for suggesting that Xinjiang be granted more autonomy*

But does all this really explain the camps? Even when one allows for the shocking nature of the violence in 2013 and 2014, the rise of Xi and the centrality of the region to China's economic future, building an entirely new network of detention centres seems a disproportionate response, even for an authoritarian state such as China.

As such, it indicates a qualitative shift in how the Communist Party views the "problem" of Xinjiang. Rather than targeting specific groups with mass arrests, and the rest of the population with propaganda – as had been the way throughout the 1990s and the 2000s – the current set of policies is aimed at the entire Muslim population of Xinjiang. Officials have been far from shy about admitting that their approach has shifted. One official in Kashgar was reported as saying: "You can't uproot all the weeds hidden among the crops in the field one by one – you need to spray chemicals to kill them all; re-educating these people is like spraying chemicals on the crops… that is why it is a general re-education, not limited to a few people."

The decision to target an entire ethnic group suggests that the Chinese government views Uighurs as inherently predisposed towards "religious extremism", or at the very least that their culture and identity makes them susceptible. While the government makes much of valuing its 55 ethnic minorities, who account for about 8% of the population, for the most part their role within contemporary Chinese culture has been confined to that →

Some officials have questioned whether Uighurs can claim to be considered part of the history of the region

→ of exotic, colourful figures who know their place within the pecking order of the nation, in which Han Chinese have precedence.

The modern notion of Han racial and cultural superiority has some of its roots in the ideas of Sun Yat-sen, the president who, in 1924, described the Han as the "single, pure race" of the Chinese nation, and argued that "the dying out of all names of individual people inhabiting China, such as Manchus, Tibetans etc," was a necessary step to forming a unified nation. In 1957, premier Zhou Enlai described assimilation as "a progressive act if it means the natural merger of nations [ie, ethnic groups] advancing towards prosperity". Three years later, Wang Enmao, the top official in Xinjiang, spoke of the need for "the complete blending of all the nationalities".

While the Chinese Communist Party is a far from monolithic entity and, like all other political bodies, contains different factions, versions of this assimilationist argument have been frequently articulated by officials and intellectuals during the communist era. The central idea was that the poverty in regions such as Xinjiang and Tibet could best be explained by the intellectual and cultural backwardness of their inhabitants, one of the chief markers of which was not speaking Mandarin. What the current set of policies in Xinjiang reveal is a belief that Uighur culture and identity is not just an obstacle to "progress" but is also actively pathological. Hence one religious affairs official advised that the camps should "break their lineage, break their roots, break their connections and break their origins".

In November 2018, Cui Tiankai, China's ambassador to the USA, said that the aim of the camps was to turn Uighurs and other Muslim minorities "into normal persons [who] can go back to normal life".

The camps are only one of the means by which this is being achieved. Arabic writing has been removed from shop fronts, street signs and packaging. In many bookstores in the region there are no longer Uighur-language instruction materials for students. Several hundred academics, musicians and writers – many of whom were previously state-sponsored – have been arrested. Not content with razing Uighur neighbourhoods throughout the region – most infamously Kashgar's Old City – the design and furnishing of Uighur homes has also come under attack, with some officials pressuring residents to change their homes to create a "new atmosphere" more in line with homes elsewhere in China.

Were this not enough, some officials have questioned whether Uighurs can claim to be considered part of the history of the region (which, according to official Chinese historiography, has always been part of China – an idea born solely of nationalism rather than historical evidence). In August 2018, the mayor of Urumqi proposed that "the Uighur people are members of the Chinese family, not descendants of the Turks, let alone anything to do with Turkish people". In September 2020, Xi repeated this notion in a speech in which he stated that "every ethnic group of Xinjiang is a family member linked to Chinese bloodlines". The idea that Uighurs are biologically part of the wider Chinese nation is perhaps the ultimate form of denial of their separate history, culture and identity.

When one considers Chinese policy in the region in toto, it amounts to cultural genocide. Judging by the present indicators, the state will not be satisfied until Uighurs are secular, Mandarin-speaking citizens who barely recognise themselves. ⊗

Nick Holdstock *is a journalist and writer who has spent many years in China. He is the author of two books about Xinjiang:* China's Forgotten People *and* The Tree That Bleeds

How to challenge China

From the passage of the National Security Law in Hong Kong to increasing evidence of genocide of Uighurs in Xinjiang, how we use our voice in the face of China's human rights abuses has never felt more important. Four people who have experience of censorship from China offer their advice

49(04): 61/63 | DOI: 10.1177/0306422020981278

TOM TUGENDHAT

Tom Tugendhat is a British Conservative Party MP who has served as chairman of the House of Commons foreign affairs committee since 2017. In April 2020, Tugendhat became the first head of the China Research Group, which has the aim of gaining a "better understanding of China's economic ambitions and global role". Several months later, he received a threatening letter sent from Hong Kong to his home address – a practice we have previously reported on (see 47.03, p102-104). He says that states must reaffirm the universality of human rights, through sanctions and joint action, in order to challenge China's human rights abuses.

FOR MORE THAN 70 years, international rules have given stability to a disorderly world. A patchwork of agreements, treaties and culture has held nations together on issues ranging from international trade to humanitarian law. The rules have channelled great power competition and sought solutions to problems faced by all.

The norms we have established have guided states in what rights they owe their citizens. The accompanying institutions have helped lift the voices of smaller nations in international forums and the principles laid down by powerful advocates like China's PC Chang have established principles we all recognise.

But those same principles are now challenged by nations that no longer see the benefit of structures and instead focus on power.

China has begun harassing smaller neighbouring states, trying to get them to concede territory and erode the principle of freedom of navigation that underpins the Law of the Sea. It is challenging the ideas of sovereignty that have established borders and boundaries and weakening the ties that bind the global economy together.

The Belt and Road Initiative has led many nations into new debt relationships that have seen them turn away from democratic freedoms and instead back policies that enable state control. This shift is dangerous at the best of times and raises all manner of questions during a time of global volatility and uncertainty.

Even within its own borders, the Communist Party is challenging our ability to respond and to uphold the systems that have served us so well.

Breaches of the Sino-British Joint Declaration undermine the rights of Hongkongers and remind us that international agreements are only as effective as our ability to police them.

And in a horrifying echo of past atrocities we'd promised never to repeat, the Communist Party's mass incarceration of Uighurs and other ethnic minorities is a test of our resolve to defend the universality of human rights. The accusations of slavery and sterilisation only demand greater investigation.

Seeing this challenge, Britain's response must be to rally support among like-minded nations. We must safeguard the principles that matter most and work out new solutions among partners with whom we can rebuild the supporting architecture of the global order where current mechanisms fail.

That will demand a range of skills from our diplomats and ministers. From building free trade agreements with those who share our principles and commit to playing fair, to agreeing to support each other in speaking out in international forums, we must reaffirm the universality of human rights, through sanctions and joint action.

Only by responding together, and through building a mutually reinforced network of states, can we be as powerful as the largest of nations.

This is not about dominance – it's about maintaining our own security by joining with others who share our values. It's not about challenging others but about defending what matters to us.

Foreign policy is about the happiness and prosperity of the British people. The past 70 years have shown us that's best delivered by defending the rules we have written together.

→

LOKMAN TSUI

Lokman Tsui is a scholar and activist, and currently an assistant professor at the School of Journalism and Communication at the Chinese University of Hong Kong, where his research focuses on free expression, digital rights and internet policy. After being involved in the pro-democracy movement in Hong Kong, he recently found out that he would not make tenure. He calls for solidarity and attention to help raise the profile of the abuses in his city.

HOW CAN YOU help Hong Kong? That was never an easy question to answer, and now it's even harder after the passing of the National Security Law. Amongst other things, the new law specifically criminalises acts that could fall under the ambiguous but broad umbrella of "foreign interference". Unsurprisingly, this has caused many international friends to freeze up when it comes to helping Hong Kong in its struggle for freedom, for fear of endangering either themselves or those of us on the ground. We are told that our struggle for freedom is illegal. We are told that the political repression we experience is normal ("every country has a national security law"). We are told that everyone else should mind their own business ("stop interfering in our domestic affairs").

So, let me ask again, how can you help Hong Kong? Look after us and pay attention to what is going on. This might sound simple but don't underestimate its impact. Knowing we are not alone, knowing that the world cares and is watching us – this is what helps keep us going. Your attention not only sustains us, it also keeps us safe. It is when the world is not paying attention that the Communist Party can run amok, as it does in Tibet and Xinjiang.

When Beijing and the Hong Kong governments tell you that "this is normal, mind your own business", say loudly and clearly that you disagree: "No, this is not normal, and no, we are not going to mind our own business." This might come at a cost, as Daryl Morey from the Houston Rockets found out when he tweeted an image with a caption saying "Fight for freedom. Stand with Hong Kong". (He later backtracked following criticism from Chinese fans, sponsors and commercial partners.) It is why the suspension of Hong Kong extradition treaties by Australia, Canada, Finland, France, Germany, New Zealand, the UK and the USA are powerful; why the suspension of user data requests by tech companies, including Facebook, Google, Microsoft and Twitter, send a clear signal. These actions not only protect the rights of Hong Kong protesters but also remind the world that what is happening in Hong Kong is not normal. It is not okay.

Thank you in advance for showing that you care, for acting in solidarity with our struggle, for standing together with us. Fight for freedom, stand with Hong Kong.

RUSHAN ABBAS

Uighur-American activist and advocate from the Xinjiang Uighur Autonomous Region in China, Rushan Abbas is founder and executive director of the non-profit Campaign for Uighurs. In 2018, her sister was abducted in Urumqi, Xinjiang. Abbas says we shouldn't shy away from inflammatory language when talking about what's happening, and we should forge connections even with those we might not always agree with.

IN PURSUIT OF human rights, there necessitates a line in the sand, and our best intentions do not negate the existence of evil. Perhaps many people are loath to believe this, to the adverse of everything good that has been won in the cause of human dignity. The genocide of the Uighurs is one glaring example of this.

The Chinese regime is currently humanity's greatest threat. To call it a challenge is a gross understatement and affords it an equivalency that this monster is not deserving of. It remains difficult for many to grasp the present reality: that China does not possess a system, or a moral bottom line, that affords any consideration of including it as an equal in the international arena. Its grasp is rapidly expanding. This is not the threat of a competitor, it is the threat of a dominator. Yet the world is reluctant to fully recognise this.

Fighting this monster means we must speak inflammatory truth. Don't shy away from it. As you inflame hearts and minds, and possibly offend, remember to treat people, even those deceived by this vast foe, as potential allies.

May the light of these flames illuminate the darkness that the world is facing in the CCP. William Pickens once said: "To cheapen the lives of any group of men, cheapens the lives of all men, even our own. This is a law of human psychology, or human nature. And it will not be repealed by our wishes, nor will it be merciful to our blindness."

So let us fight our battle with the confidence that while life has many grey areas, this is not one. Be bolder than the boldest. The future of humanity depends on it.

ABOVE: Graffiti seen on a pavement during the anti-extradition bill movement in Hong Kong

ANNE-MARIE BRADY

Anne-Marie Brady is a professor at the University of Canterbury, New Zealand, specialising in Chinese politics. In September 2017, she presented a conference paper titled Magic Weapons: China's Political Influence Activities Under Xi Jinping, detailing the Communist Party's attempts to influence international opinion, with New Zealand as a case study. Following the paper's release, her university office and home were broken into. Interpol has been involved in the investigation to see who was behind it. Here, she calls for more accountability and transparency in dealing with China.

THE CHINESE COMMUNIST Party efforts to interfere in foreign politics are like water on limestone: it will find the cracks and weak spots in each society. Governments need to develop their own holistic, non-partisan approach to dealing with this issue, to respond to the CCP's "whole of party" effort in political interference activities. Governments should strengthen anti-corruption measures, such as bringing in comprehensive laws against corruption and to manage lobbying activities, conflicts of interest and money-laundering.

Governments should also assess legislation around political donations. Political parties should be required to carry out due diligence on all donations. Governments should pass legislation to register agents of foreign governments. Politicians should not be members of foreign political parties or simultaneously of two local political parties. National and local government representatives should not be permitted to join, promote or act on behalf of CCP united front organisations.

The public should be informed on the challenges as well as the opportunities of China relations. Society has an important role in national security; an informed society is the means to engage in total defence. Our democracies are at a pivotal moment as they respond to a complex new security environment. Confronting the issue of foreign interference is a difficult matter for any state. The strategic order is shifting and governments must adjust their foreign policies.

The political parties in each democracy must come together, without recrimination, to address the issue of the CCP's interference in the political system. The way forward is to jointly 1) establish a non-partisan resilience strategy; 2) exchange information and seek support from other like-minded states and sister political parties; 3) focus on common points with China while facing up to the differences and challenges in the wider relationship; and 4) craft joint, multi-nation statements on issues of concern, such as the human rights situation in Hong Kong and Xinjiang.

Abuse not part of journalist's day job

A journalist in the Netherlands has won a landmark trial against online abusers, reports **Fréderike Geerdink**

CLARICE GARGARD HAS just emerged from a two-year court case against the people who sent racist and sexist slurs as she was live-streaming an anti-racism protest. Now the journalist and author says she needs some peace and quiet – at least until the end of the year.

On her Instagram account she said she was taking a break, including pausing her regular column in the daily paper NRC Handelsblad, posting: "Public life … doesn't sustain me. The ability to create does, and when there is no space there is little place to create."

The American-Dutch journalist, whose roots are in Liberia, is finally exhaling, as she called it on Instagram, after a court case against the people who harassed her online ended in the Netherlands.

The case, which was wrapped up in November, lasted two years. The result was that 24 people were convicted of incitement, insult and discrimination and sentenced to fines of up to €450 and up to 58 hours' community service. One person was acquitted.

The comments, which included death threats and calls to kill demonstrators, did not directly incite violence but the court said that they "could very well have spurred someone on to take action". It was the first time that online hate against a journalist was taken to court on this scale in the Netherlands.

Those tried were part of an online mob that attacked Gargard in November 2018 as she took part in a demonstration against Zwarte Piet, the blackface caricature that accompanies St Nicholas on his annual visit to the Netherlands before Christmas.

Gargard, who is known for her sharp anti-racist writing and speaking, went to the protest out of solidarity and to possibly write about it. When she started live-streaming the event on Facebook, the vile comments came flowing in.

In the interview on Dutch public radio after the judges' ruling, Gargard said: "Initially I thought that I was used to this as a columnist and as somebody who speaks out against racism. Only after the protest, when I came home, I saw how bad the comments were. I was shocked. But I wasn't sure what to do."

She added: "There were some 8,000 messages and they were so threatening, so full of hate, so racist, sexist, homophobic, such a rich mix of everything. It was crossing the line. I could no longer accept this: not just for myself but also for others who have to experience this, other journalists, activists, women, people of colour. It just has to stop."

Friends encouraged her to press charges. At the time, journalists' union NVJ had just launched an initiative in co-operation with editors, the police and the public prosecutor to give more priority to tackling threats and violence against journalists. The initiative, called PersVeilig (PressSafe), was triggered by increasing physical violence against journalists in the Netherlands, as well as online hate.

Thomas Bruning, general secretary of the NVJ, told Index: "Gargard's case was exemplary for what we want to tackle. We contacted

> *There were some 8,000 messages and they were so threatening, so full of hate, so racist, sexist, homophobic, such a rich mix of everything. It was crossing the line*

ABOVE: The journalist Clarice Gargard

the prosecutor, pressuring them not to leave this case collecting dust in a drawer. When they said it was a complex case and that it would take time, we urged them to keep Gargard informed so she wouldn't think she had pressed charges in vain."

That was important, Bruning explained, because journalists often assume that threats, racism and intimidation cannot be fought judicially, that the police are not equipped enough and that the cases are too complicated.

"It is important to show that the public prosecutor does pick it up," he said. "Not only for the journalists involved but also for the people who attack them. They have to know they won't get away with it."

Online hate, racism and sexism are, in other words, not part of the job.

In one of her columns for NRC Handelsblad, Gargard mentioned the support she received from the paper. Deputy editor-in-chief Elske Schouten told Index it was significant that people were being attacked so viciously because of who they were and that Gargard "received so much garbage as a black woman".

She added: "It needs to stop."

But even though Bruning sees the case's outcome as being a victory, he said that it took too long: "She could have started recovering sooner if the case had not taken two years. The mental burden could have been lighter." ⊗

Fréderike Geerdink is a freelance journalist who writes about power and those who want to break it down. She is based in both the Netherlands and Kurdistan

Two faces of On Liberty

There's an intolerance in the new liberalism.
John Gray asks if John Stuart Mill is to blame

49(04): 66/69 | DOI: 10.1177/0306422020981280

IT IS TEMPTING to think the rise of intolerance can be countered by a return to classical liberal principles. The move to censorship that has occurred in universities, publishing houses, museums and other cultural institutions marks a clear breach with freedom of expression as defined by liberals in the past. Those who defend the practice of "cancelling" speakers, writers and works of art do so on the grounds that they may be offensive. Yet a key feature of liberalism has been that offence to others cannot by itself justify curbs on freedom of expression.

The point of free expression is to enable free inquiry, which includes the unfettered play of the imagination in the arts. This freedom to explore and question may generate psychological discomfort. One of the functions of free expression is to confront us with awkward realities. But according to the version of liberalism that now prevails, it seems, avoiding mental distress should trump the pursuit of truth.

Autonomous people do not automatically internalise the norms of their society. They fashion their values for themselves, making and remaking them

The old-fashioned liberal view is nowhere better presented than in John Stuart Mill's Essay on Liberty (1859). The core of Mill's argument has to do with fallibility. Since all our beliefs are prone to error, they need challenging in open debate. In theory, Mill applied this argument to every field of human knowledge. According to his System of Logic (1843), even the truths of mathematics might have to be revised in light of experience and discussion. Nothing could be insulated from criticism.

In practice, Mill's recognition of human fallibility did not extend to his own moral beliefs. For him, it was axiomatic that the best life was self-chosen. Inherited ways of living might contain good things. Traditional religions had in some ways contributed to human wellbeing, for example. But human beings achieved the best of what they were capable only when the lives they led expressed what Mill called "individuality"– their unique needs and possibilities – which could be discovered only by making their own choices. Any life based on tradition or convention was essentially hostile to human progress. As Mill put it: "The despotism of custom is everywhere the standing hindrance to human advancement, being in unceasing antagonism to that disposition to aim at something better than customary, which is called, according to circumstances, the spirit of liberty, or that of progress and improvement."

By individuality, Mill meant what we nowadays call personal autonomy. Autonomous individuals do not live by received rules of behaviour. They engage in what Mill called "experiments of living", improvising new forms of life they believe may suit them better than any they have inherited. An autonomous person does not automatically internalise the norms of their society. They fashion their values for themselves, making and remaking them as they try different ways of living. Mill did this himself, when he engaged in an irregular relationship with a married woman, the feminist writer Harriet Taylor. The experiment appears to have been successful, despite the disapproval of Victorian society, since the two seem to →

IN FOCUS

VANITY FAIR

→ have enjoyed a happy life together after they married when her husband died.

Mill's defence of individuality expresses a strong strand in modern culture. In the Romantic tradition, by which he was much influenced in his youth, originality was regarded as the supreme value in art. For Mill it was also the key to the good life. Human beings should create themselves as artists (the Romantics believed) created their works. Only then would they be truly happy.

There are some problems with this modern ideal. Many may feel the need to create a way of living for themselves, but nearly all human beings have other needs as well. Most of them need the sense of security that comes with settled relationships in families and communities. Certainly, they want the freedom to exit when their relationships turn sour. That does not mean they value their personal autonomy over all other values.

Officially, Mill always remained a utilitarian, following the creed his father taught him. For James Mill and his mentor Jeremy Bentham, the greatest happiness – which for them meant the maximal satisfaction of human wants – was all that mattered. But the author of On Liberty knew that following this utilitarian philosophy had not made him happy. In early adulthood, he suffered devastating depression when he asked himself whether it would be a great joy to him if all of the world-improving changes in society he yearned for could be achieved in an instant. "An irrepressible self-consciousness distinctly answered: 'No!' At this my heart sank: the whole foundation on which my life was constructed fell down."

Mill spent the rest of his days trying to revise the utilitarian conception of happiness so that it took full account of individuality. On Liberty was one of the products of this attempt. However, as he refined the idea of happiness to make it accord with his own life, his version of utilitarianism became less and less based on fact and experience. For Mill, the higher pleasures that come with developing one's unique nature counted more than any others. Through an intellectual sleight of hand, happiness became one and the same with individuality.

> *Human beings should create themselves as artists (the Romantics believed) created their works. Only then would they be truly happy*

At this point Mill abandoned any idea of fallibility. That a rational human being will prefer higher over lower pleasures was not a conclusion he reached by observation of humankind. It was a necessary truth, no doubt grounded in his own experience, but unfalsifiable by contrary evidence. Here we find the germ of the liberal intolerance that is currently in vogue.

The idea that the good life must be self-created underpins the now common belief that everyone must be schooled in autonomous choice. It is not enough to be protected from coercion as older types of liberalism demanded. Such negative liberty would leave people subject to what Mill called the despotism of custom. A more positive kind of freedom had to be inculcated – one that empowered people to fashion their lives and identities for themselves.

Personal autonomy is a legitimate and, in some ways, attractive ideal. But it is only one among many visions of the good life that human beings cherish and pursue, and when it becomes dominant in public institutions it can create a climate of intolerance as strong as that against which Mill revolted in Victorian England, if not more so. The oppression against which Mill railed was chiefly that of gossip directed at his relationship with Harriet Taylor. Today, the penalty for nonconformity can be loss of livelihood.

There is another kind of intolerance in the new liberalism. Inevitably, much of humankind will be regarded as backward. If you are a traditionalist Christian, Orthodox Jew or strictly practising Muslim, you will be seen as lagging behind in the grand march of progress. If, like many people, you aim simply to muddle along without any fixed idea of the good life, you risk being regarded as unworthy of freedom.

Here the new liberals follow Mill, who made clear that for him liberty was not an intrinsic good. Its value was in its contribution to utility, "but it must be utility in the largest sense, grounded on the permanent interests of man as a progressive being". In other words, liberty could be curbed whenever it stood in the way of progress. Those who resist progress are not merely backward. By disregarding "the permanent interests of man", they show they are less than fully human. For liberals who think this way, limiting the freedom of expression of enemies of progress has an irresistible logic.

What Mill called "the spirit of liberty" does not always coincide with that of "progress and improvement". He was able to avoid this conflict because he believed free expression would, over the long run, promote his ideal of individuality. But this belief was not a result of scientific inquiry, and what he expected has not come to pass. There are many ready to trade off autonomy for negative liberty, or else for security.

There are also many who reject the ideal of autonomy. For them, happiness means belonging in an enduring way of life. Rather than

looking for self-realisation in experiments in living, they find fulfilment in deep commitments. A free society must have room for these people as much as for those who prize personal autonomy. Both deserve freedom and respect. The aim of a more pluralistic liberalism should be to devise a modus vivendi that both can accept.

On Liberty may present the canonical argument for freedom of expression, but it also contains the seeds of the threat to free expression at the present time. Returning to Mill is no way out from today's illiberal liberalism, for it was part of Mill's liberalism that began this intolerant creed. ⊗

The idea that the good life must be self-created underpins the now common belief that everyone must be schooled in autonomous choice

John Gray *is an English political philosopher. He is the author of Mill on Liberty: A Defence and Two Faces of Liberalism*

Out with the old?

Rumours, lies, denials and intimidation all played prominent roles in the 2020 presidential election campaign and its aftermath. But Trump's tactics were far from unusual in US history, writes **Robert Speel**

49(04): 70/72 | DOI: 10.1177/0306422020981281

FALSE CLAIMS OF discarded ballots, people outside polling stations with guns, a president unwilling to concede defeat and, of course, lies, lies and more lies – all of these defined the 2020 US election as part of a campaign to discredit the truth alongside the very heart of democracy. Such tactics may have seemed extreme in 2020, but they are not new to US presidential campaigns. As early as 1800, John Adams was accused during his re-election bid of trying to arrange a marriage between his son and a daughter of King George III in order to create a unified bloodline and reunite the two countries. Then, in the 1828 race between his son, John Quincy Adams, and Andrew Jackson, Jackson's late mother was accused of having been a prostitute who engaged in sexual relations with a mixed-race man who fathered Jackson, while Jackson's wife was accused of bigamy.

But the smears went both ways. John Quincy Adams, who had been president since 1825, was labelled a pimp. In fact, many voters felt he should not have been president to begin with. During the election of 1824, Jackson had won the popular vote but not the electoral-college vote, and the election had been decided by the House of Representatives. A man called Henry Clay supported Adams and, in return, was made secretary of state. Jackson's supporters labelled this "the corrupt bargain" and spent the next four years calling Adams a usurper.

In a more recent election, investigations into the Watergate scandal revealed that the Richard Nixon re-election campaign of 1972 involved a "dirty tricks" squad, whose job was to sabotage the campaigns of Democratic opponents by spreading false rumours and playing pranks.

While social media and the internet have exacerbated the problem of lies and intimidation, such tactics have always existed in some form in US political campaigns. What is new is a president who directly promotes conspiracy theories, with almost half of the public supporting him.

As for voter intimidation, that too has a long history. During the mid-19th century, the practice of "cooping" became widespread, in which paid partisan gangs would kidnap voters, keep them prisoner while plying them with alcohol, and then take them to a large number of polling places in order to stuff the ballot boxes with fraudulent votes. Some historians have written that author Edgar Allan Poe was a victim of such a scheme.

Following the American Civil War in the 1860s, methods of voter intimidation only got worse, particularly in southern

BELOW: President Lyndon B Johnson signs the 1965 Voting Rights Act surrounded by Martin Luther King, Clarence Mitchell Jr. and Rosa Parks. The act outlawed discriminatory voting practices

states where white supremacists tried every tactic possible to prevent the newly enfranchised African-Americans from voting. During the 1876 presidential election, widespread intimidation led to disputed election results in three states and the "compromise of 1877", in which southern Democrats allowed a Republican to be elected president in return for northern military troops leaving the South.

Soon after, southern states enacted practices such as literacy tests and poll taxes to prevent almost all African-Americans in the South from being able to vote. For those who tried, white supremacist militias would threaten or exercise violence outside polling places.

Later that century, most states adopted the "Australian ballot" (so named because it had been first used in parts of Australia). These ballots were produced by the government rather than political parties and allowed votes to be cast secretly to end practices such as cooping. They also made voter intimidation and bribery more difficult. Further positive change came in the 1960s when the US constitution was amended to ban poll taxes, and in 1965 Congress passed the Voting Rights Act to ban literacy tests and send federal authorities to southern states to prevent intimidation at polling places.

The 2000 presidential election featured a remnant of Florida's voter intimidation laws against African-Americans. The state procured a database of people allegedly convicted of felonies in other states who now lived in Florida (and therefore would lose their right to vote for life under Florida law at the time). Most of the names in the database were of African-Americans, and the database was filled with errors. Many of them were prevented from voting in the election.

Immediately after the election, Republicans labelled Democrat Al Gore's request for a hand count of uncounted ballots as demands for "recounts", as if Gore were being a sore loser. In fact, Gore was requesting that ballots that had been left uncounted by punch-card reading machines be looked at manually to determine what voters had intended.

The mess of that election led to a ban on punch-card ballots throughout the USA and the adoption of more modern voting technologies, as well as a new emphasis on early voting and postal ballots to prevent all errors in the voting process from occurring on just one day.

"Jackson is to be President, and you will be HANGED."

ABOVE: A political cartoon showing Andrew Jackson hanging John Quincy Adams, who he defeated in the 1828 election

> Investigations into the Watergate scandal revealed that the Richard Nixon re-election campaign of 1972 involved a "dirty tricks" squad

ROUGHING UP A SMOOTH TRANSITION

With the departing US president having one month left in office, **BENJAMIN LYNCH** asks just how much damage he can do

THE TRANSITION PERIOD is one of the more remarkable features of US democracy. A president who in some cases loses an election can remain in power for two whole months before his successor moves into the White House.

Though it appears to have originated because of the difficulty early presidents faced in getting to Washington DC, the protracted handover of power is now seen as a way of giving a sense of continuity and stability. Will this be the case under Donald Trump?

In an interview with Index, Joseph A Russomanno, professor of media law and the First Amendment at Arizona State University, said there was a tradition of exiting US presidents not doing too much during transition periods. But he added: "Donald Trump is known for rejecting tradition. Anything is possible."

The last two months of a presidency are known as the "lame duck" period, with outgoing incumbents exercising little real power.

The system relies heavily on precedent and on a gracious showing of support despite there perhaps being key differences with the incoming president. This happened when George W Bush signed off on a $350 billion bailout during the 2008-09 financial crisis as he prepared to hand over the reins to the incoming Barack Obama.

Russomanno spoke of the importance of a smooth transition. Yet so far Trump has shown few signs of wanting this to happen and has of course questioned the validity of the ballot itself – the very cornerstone of democracy and free expression.

And his worrying record on media freedom over the course of his presidency doesn't bode well for his last few weeks in office.

"The door that has been open to him with regard to press freedom and limiting it is still open. It is open until the day he leaves office," Russomanno said.

As for the next president, Joe Biden, it will be just as important for the media to remain impartial and critical as it has been under Trump.

"With a Democrat in the White House, the thinking will be that the press favours him," said Russomanno. "The notion of fairness is paramount. If there is a burden on the news media after Biden takes office, it will be to demonstrate that they are watchdogs on him and his administration in the same way as they were on Trump's administration."

→ The federal Help America Vote Act of 2002 requires states to allow provisional ballots at polling places for voters who believe they are allowed to vote but who encounter an administrative obstacle, to allow election officials to check afterwards whether such voters have a legal right to vote.

In 2018, Florida voters approved an amendment to the state constitution to restore voting rights to convicted felons other than those who had been convicted for murder or violent sexual offences. That said, change is not always linear: in 2019, the Florida state legislature approved a law to restrict restoration of voting rights to those who had paid all fees and fines associated with their convictions and court hearings, which can be expensive for lower-income ex-convicts in Florida.

It's not clear what the political future of Trump or his movement will be. For the next four years, the USA will probably not have a president who publicly promotes conspiracy theories and calls for intimidation of the supporters of his political opponents. But many fear that the political tactics promoted by Trump will not end even when his presidency does – and history doesn't necessarily put minds at ease. ⊗

The 2000 presidential election featured a remnant of Florida's voter intimidation laws

Robert Speel is associate professor of political science at Penn State Erie, The Behrend College

The Sudanese revolution will be illustrated

Sudanese artist **Khalid Albaih** says his cartoons start conversations. He's got his friends, and his enemies, he tells **Abraham T Zere**

49(04): 73/75 | DOI: 10.1177/0306422020981282

MERELY FOR BEING a political cartoonist, Khalid Albaih has been called "an enemy of the state". Coming from the Middle East and North Africa, where leaders often hold on to power for life and pass it down to their relatives, challenging authority is unavoidable for cartoonists such as Albaih.

"My job is to critique the government, to critique the system, to critique the society in a simple way that's accessible by most people," he told Index from his home in Copenhagen, where he is an International Cities of Refuge Network artist in residence.

"Authoritarian regimes survive and exist through fear. So when you mock fear, you break their persona and their means of survival. By doing so, you're giving a sign to people that 'If I can mock these, so can you'."

Born in 1980 in Romania, where his father was a diplomat, and raised in Sudan, where his uncle Abdel Rahman Suwar al-Dahab was president, Albaih fled the country in 1990 with his family after Omar Hassan al-Bashir seized power through a military coup.

He started drawing early on, doing his own comic strips at school, then moving to more political cartoons during university. But after university he struggled to find work in traditional media. Albaih, who now calls himself a "virtual revolutionist", decided instead to publish online. And the timing could not have been more fortuitous, happening just as the Arab Spring occurred, which saw online tools driving the revolutionary zeal. Soon his work went viral and was also painted on walls, from Tahrir Square to Beirut.

Unlike many, Albaih remains optimistic about the Arab Spring. The French Revolution, he argues, took generations to exert its full impact. The Middle East and North Africa is still at an intermediate stage of revolution. Despite the failure of peaceful power transitions in many countries after the popular uprisings, Albaih has observed one promising development. He believes the revolution changed the perception of citizens and challenged the status quo for the first time in years.

"It gave the people hope and introduced the term 'revolution'," he said.

ABOVE & RIGHT: Sudanese artist Khalid Albaih. On top of political cartoons, Albaih often critiques social media

→ But he added that he hadn't "slept well for the last 10 years" when asked how much time he devoted to the cause at the height of the uprising, including later when revolution came to his home country.

Albaih went to Sudan after the ousting of al-Bashir, which happened in April 2019. He became one of the most vocal people documenting the revolution of 2018-19 and has used his platform and public profile to try to inform the world about what is happening there.

"For 30 years, al-Bashir and his minions broke the hopes of everyone," Albaih said. "They enabled this by letting nobody else grow. By popularising the idea that we are failures, they inculcated the feeling that no one can rule."

Then suddenly the nation realised that it didn't need one charismatic ruler or even a recognisable leader. The Sudanese Professional Association, a loose trade-union collective that spearheaded the Sudanese Revolution, showed the way.

After al-Bashir, Albaih has been happy with some developments. He witnessed a vibrant atmosphere where people felt safe to voice their opinions and talk freely without fear of reprisals. He watched as activists debated on TV, a concept that had been absent for decades.

"Freedom of speech is really what this revolution has brought back to the Sudanese mind," he said.

Yet he does not conceal his fears regarding the volatile region. He hopes people will cherish what they have and fight to defend it, and acknowledges this might be tough. Some regional powers he believes have an interest in not seeing democracy in Sudan. He fears countries like the UAE, Saudi Arabia and Egypt could try to create chaos and limit free speech.

"So we're not fighting only for the freedom of Sudan but for the region at large," he said.

Amongst Albaih's best known work is his illustration of the American football player Colin Kaepernick, whose decision to kneel in protest at

> *Freedom of speech is really what this revolution has brought back to the Sudanese mind*

BELOW: A cartoon from October 2020 ahead of the US election

police brutality against black people sparked major controversy and continues to stir strong opinions. The Kaepernick illustration was praised and promoted by, among others, prominent black film director Spike Lee.

While he receives lots of positive feedback, not everyone is a fan of his work. In countries such as the UAE and Saudi Arabia, publicly engaging with Albaih's work can get you in serious trouble.

His Facebook fan page, called Khartoon!, which has more than 85,000 followers, often entertains heated discussions. Albaih is no stranger to being trolled, being threatened or called names such as "George Soros's agent".

"You can't tell if all these people are employed primarily to do that or sincerely believe what they write," he said.

Admirers who support his work must write to him privately. And many do.

Whether artists hail from repressive regimes or more democratic countries, Albaih says their role is to initiate a conversation. He does not think he can change people's minds through his work but he strives to show different perspectives and enrich the discussion – which is exactly what he did in an exhibition he held last year in the USA. As a Muslim and a foreigner, whose country was proposed for inclusion in the "Muslim travel ban" by the US administration, he visited to critique president Donald Trump's "Mexico wall". Where did he go? White-majority and Republican-dominated Jacksonville, Florida. In his exhibition in July 2019, dubbed "Camp/ Wall/ Flock", he divided the museum in half. Visitors could choose to watch the passports that were held captive on one side or flying passports – suspended in the air – that crossed the wall on the other.

Asked if he faced a backlash as a Muslim and a person of colour, he laughed. "It started the conversation and made people talk."

Khalid Albaih (inspired by a cartoon by BRANCH)

ABOVE: Albaih, who often draws cartoons on Sudan, returned to the country last year to document the revolution

> *Authoritarian regimes survive and exist through fear. So when you mock fear, you break their persona and their means of survival*

Abraham T Zere *is a US-based Eritrean exiled journalist and writer*

THE DEBATE

Social media platforms have a moral duty to ban misinformation about vaccines

Ahead of a Covid-19 vaccine becoming widely available, two leading thinkers go head-to-head to debate the moral implications of allowing fake news to flourish versus censoring it

49(04): 76/79 I DOI: 10.1177/0306422020981283

Jonathan Kennedy:

YES Vaccines have had arguably the greatest positive impact of any technology ever invented by humans. Immunisation programmes have eradicated or radically reduced the incidence of some of the most deadly and devastating infectious diseases. The World Health Organization estimates that vaccines save 2-3 million lives every year. It should come as no surprise, therefore, that our greatest hope for ending the death and disruption caused by Covid-19 is to develop a vaccine.

Despite the remarkable public health benefits of vaccines, a significant proportion of the population views them with hostility and suspicion. These feelings are largely driven by unsubstantiated concerns that governments, pharmaceutical companies and public health authorities are hiding evidence of vaccines' dangerous side-effects.

Low vaccine confidence is not a new issue, but it has received a great deal of attention over the last few months because it threatens to undermine future efforts to end the Covid-19 pandemic. According to the Pew Center, almost half of Americans would "probably not" or "definitely not" get the Covid-19 vaccine if and when one becomes available. While the figures are not as high in the UK, they are still alarming: in a study conducted by King's College London of attitudes to having a possible Covid-19 vaccine, 10% answered "I would not" and 19% "Don't know".

Social media has transformed the way that people communicate and access information. As a recent article in The Lancet pointed out, social media offers "an unprecedented opportunity to amplify and spread anti-vaccination messages". Half of British parents with children under five have seen negative messages about vaccines on social media, according to the Royal Society for Public Health. The current pandemic poses an existential threat to the world as we know it. We must consider every available option to increase confidence in vaccines – and this includes prohibiting misinformation on social media.

Julie Leask:

NO The impact of vaccines is indisputable, despite opposition to vaccination stretching back to Edward Jenner's first experiments. Social media censorship, however, is not the solution to challenges surrounding uptake, and comes with some concerning consequences. In short, the basis for censoring anti-vaccination messages in social media is flawed, the process is prone to error and the outcomes can be perilous.

I will begin with the flawed basis of censorship. Calls to censor misinformation rest on a hypodermic model of influence where information is "injected" into the passive mind of an individual who then acts in response. Yet studies consistently find that people are influenced to vaccinate by how they think and feel. They are particularly influenced by the people and institutions in their lives; and practical issues, such as vaccine availability and convenient and culturally appropriate services. Parents who actively refuse vaccines describe beliefs, experiences with healthcare and parenting practices as pivotal to their decisions.

Social media is a mode of communication but we lack evidence that the misinformation alone is influential enough to cause a population impact on vaccination coverage, though this is often claimed. Global vaccination coverage has increased, not declined, over the past 20 years and since social media has become widely used. A recent global survey found just six out of 149 countries had a significant increase in the percentage of respondents strongly disagreeing that vaccines were safe, with the largest increases in Azerbaijan, Serbia and Pakistan. Perceptions of safety, or of the effectiveness or importance of vaccines, were weakly associated with uptake. For Covid-19, a recent study showed intentions to vaccinate at a country level were strongly influenced by trust in government.

Vaccines are based on sound science. The process for achieving high vaccination uptake should also be based on sound evidence.

Kennedy:
YES The rise in global vaccination coverage over the past 20 years is not primarily driven by changing attitudes. Rather, it is a consequence of massive amounts of money spent on improving access to vaccines in low and middle-income countries by organisations such as GAVI, the Vaccine Alliance.

In high-income countries, there is evidence that vaccine uptake has fallen in response to fears about safety. For example, the percentage of children receiving the MMR vaccine in the UK and the USA is lower now than in 1998, when Andrew Wakefield published his fraudulent research linking MMR with autism.

It should be noted that authors of the global survey that Professor Leask cites pointed out that the marked falls in vaccine confidence in South Korea and Malaysia were caused by "online mobilisation against vaccines". The same study stated that misinformation about the HPV vaccine that began in Japan spread throughout the world via "online media and social media networks".

Attitudes to vaccines can be conceptualised as a spectrum. At one end are people who accept that vaccines are safe and effective. →

→ At the other extreme are the non-believers – so-called anti-vaxxers. It is unlikely that misinformation would affect either group's deeply entrenched convictions. This is not the case for the "fence-sitters" located in the middle of the spectrum who are unsure about the risks and benefits of vaccination.

It is true that the relationship between social media misinformation and attitudes to vaccines is not well understood by researchers. This doesn't mean that no such link exists. Advertisers paid Facebook almost $70 billion in 2019 precisely because social media has the power to shape our mood, beliefs and behaviour – although systemic absorption strikes me as a more apt medical metaphor for how this happens than hypodermic injection.

Leask:

NO It is true that safety issues can sometimes lower vaccination rates, but censoring social media misinformation will not be an effective response. Open communication can build the trust on which effective vaccination programmes rely.

Censorship will also backfire. A core appeal of anti-vaccination claims has long been the cover-up of negative information for conspiratorial purposes. To censor plays into this narrative and risks attracting a broader coalition of voices who reject attempts by powerful actors to control what people see. In doing so, censorship will give anti-vaccination activists and their misinformation more, not less, attention.

The process of censorship is also prone to error. Censors must find a reasonable dividing line between truth and falsehood in a complex field. Insufficiently-qualified censors may place thresholds for censorship too high, shutting down expression of genuine concerns. With vaccines to prevent Covid-19, public hesitancy is not a pathology but a reasonable and predictable pattern when vaccines are new and final trial data is yet to be reported.

Robust vaccination programmes are secure enough to withstand some dissent. These programmes are characterised by solid primary care, co-ordinated systems and sustained funding. They offer people convenient and welcoming services. They train health professionals to be knowledgeable, skilled and confident to answer questions. Robust programmes have strong safety monitoring and adverse-events response systems. They prioritise transparent communication, trust and engagement with diverse populations. Misinformation loves a vacuum, but robust programmes fill early information gaps with open and frequent communication.

Dr Kennedy argues that safety fears caused the recent decline in the UK's childhood vaccination coverage. However, expert analysis concluded that reorganisation of health services, changed migration patterns and a reduction in vaccination reminder systems were the most likely causes. Significantly, there was a four-percentage point decrease in the proportion of parents seeing anything that might persuade them not to vaccinate.

Misinformation generates a lot of heat and noise. But we should not be distracted or dismayed: we can trust the audiences and respond with nuance, confidence and calmness.

Kennedy:

YES Before curtailing my argument, I'll reiterate an important point: online misinformation undermines vaccine confidence. Consider, for example, a study released this November by researchers from the Vaccine Confidence Project that revealed the proportion of British people willing to vaccinate themselves fell by 6.4% after they viewed vaccine misinformation online. Those who changed their minds were not hardened anti-vaxxers but fence-sitters.

Another recent study showed that people with lower numeracy skills were more likely to believe coronavirus-related misinformation. On its own, this is a cause for concern because it demonstrates that these people and their families are harmed by these untruths. But it also creates a problem for the whole of society because it can undermine the herd immunity that protects people who have not been or cannot be vaccinated, including newborn babies and children undergoing chemotherapy. The 6.4% of the population who refuse vaccines after viewing online misinformation could be

the difference between herd immunity or not.

It is interesting to consider who produces this misinformation and why. An article published in the American Journal of Public Health demonstrated that the same Russian Twitter bots and trolls that interfered with the 2016 US election on the side of Donald Trump also spread misinformation about vaccines. The authors concluded that the issue of vaccine safety was being "weaponised" by a hostile power that wanted to create social discord.

Even from a liberal perspective, there is a clear case for banning vaccine misinformation. While those who peddle untruths often defend their right to do so by invoking individual freedom, more nuanced liberals such as John Stuart Mill argue that exercising our personal freedom should not harm other people. Just like violence and hate speech, vaccine misinformation falls foul of Mill's Harm Principle. In a society that aspires to protect its members – especially those who are vulnerable – we must restrict the propagation of harmful misinformation.

Leask:
NO Public health indeed accepts limiting certain freedoms when this can be shown to bring a greater good. Mandatory seat belts, indoor smoking bans and quarantine laws are policies where infringements on personal liberties are justified by strong evidence of benefit.

A decision to limit rights to freedom of expression also needs strong support. Censorship must be done with great care, as it can cover-up both misinformation and truth. Countries using censorship as a tool of political oppression increasingly cite the need to control misinformation, implementing "fake news laws" where the bycatch can include legitimate journalism. A recent Unesco report cautioned against rapidly moving to curtailing disinformation without appropriate debate, transparency and scrutiny.

This challenging environment calls for balanced, proportionate strategies that do not erode human rights. Rather than reactively moderating content, the focus should be on keeping vaccine programmes resilient: meeting demand for information with early credible information; monitoring the sharing

The percentage of children receiving the MMR vaccine in the UK and the USA is lower now than in 1998, when Andrew Wakefield published his fraudulent research linking MMR with autism

of misinformation to see what is salient; addressing actual information needs (not assumed ones); and managing hesitancy well in healthcare situations. Countries need to support public interest journalism. Young people – the parents of tomorrow – should have sufficient digital literacy to critically view content.

While bots may account for 9%-15% of all Twitter accounts, few people follow them. This means that their vaccine-critical content is almost never seen, as our recent study found; between 2017 and 2019 in the USA, a typical Twitter user potentially saw 757 vaccine-related posts, of which 27 were critical of vaccination and less than 0.5% originated from bots.

The greatest enemies of vaccination are poverty, disadvantage, failed health systems and neglectful governments. People require opportunities and capabilities to vaccinate and this does not always happen.

Through preventing certain infectious diseases, vaccines aim to improve the wellbeing of individuals, communities and societies. The process by which vaccination is supported should not compete with this ultimate aim. ⊗

Jonathan Kennedy *is senior lecturer in global public health at Queen Mary, University of London. His research focuses on health and on vaccine hesitancy*

Julie Leask *is a professor at the Faculty of Medicine and Health, University of Sydney. Her research focuses on risk communication, and vaccine hesitancy and refusal*

MAIN: Kuwait City, 2018. Books hang from a tree outside the National Assembly in protest against censorship regulations

CULTURE

82 FIGHTING THE PROPAGANDA TSARS
SERGEY KHAZOV-CASSIA
A novel in Russian about LGBTQ has to be wrapped in plastic in order to sell. Here we speak to the author, **Sergey Khazov-Cassia,** about navigating this difficult space and why people in Russia might support the restrictive gay propaganda law. Plus an exclusive extract from it

87 BANNING THOSE WHO BAN BOTHAYNA AL-ESSA
A key censorship law that banned certain books being published and sold in Kuwait has recently been overturned. **Bothayna al-Essa** tells **Jemimah Steinfeld** why the change was so important, plus an extract from her latest book Guardian of Superficialities published in English for the first time

94 "YOUR LIMITLESS GRIEF IS A TALE WITH NO ENDING" JOSHUA L FREEMAN
The plight of the Uighurs is laid bare by three of Xinjiang's most prominent poets. We publish poems from **Abuqadir Jüme Tunyuquq, Idris Nurulla** and **Shahip Abdusalam Nurbeg**, who are all currently in China's concentration camps

Fighting the propaganda tsars

Having literature with LGBTQ themes published in Russia is almost impossible. But young people in the country need it, says **Sergey Khazov-Cassia** in an interview with **Benjamin Lynch**

49(04): 82/86 | DOI: 10.1177/0306422020981284

WHEN RUSSIA'S GAY propaganda law was introduced in 2013, it enshrined in law homophobic attitudes that were already rife in society.

Today, Russia's LGBTQ population largely keep details of their private lives quiet for fear of landing on the wrong side of the law, and journalist and author Sergey Khazov-Cassia's books are sold wrapped in plastic for the same reason. They also come with age restrictions to deter younger readers.

"It is sold in plastic wrapping so it doesn't break the law," he said. "Plastic coverings ensure the book's cover and title (which may imply the genre of literature it contains) is covered as to ensure readers are discouraged from buying it… Big bookstores didn't take this book, [but] it sold quite well through internet shops."

The Gospel According To is Khazov-Cassia's second book and deals with queer repression, discrimination but also liberation within modern Russia.

The pages published here in English for the first time are an extract from the 2016 book, where the main character discusses his HIV-positive partner's viral load – the amount of virus in an infected person's blood.

In Russia, HIV patients must reach a certain level of viral load before they begin treatment, something that goes against advice from the

World Health Organisation.

Much of the novel's theme also concerns the attitudes of Russian people towards homosexuals. The Gospel According To is – in some parts – candid in its use of sex. It is this content that Khazov-Cassia believes limits the appeal among non-LGBTQ Russians.

"This book has quite a lot of sex scenes. Some of the people helping me write the book, such as lawyers and people who work with prisons, are not LGBT at all, they are just activists, so I felt a bit red-faced about some of the content."

Although literature with gay themes has a long history in Russia (there are writings from as early as the 11th century, for example), the past century has not been favourable towards this literature and its authors. Gay Soviet writers faced persecution, and the hostility has only increased under Vladimir Putin.

The law means that Khasov-Cassia's book cannot necessarily provide gay children with answers to life's burning questions.

Pondering the lack of access to literature, contrasted with the plethora of incorrect information on harmful internet sites, he mused: "Censorship here just limits the spread of information. When I was a teenager we didn't have the internet, so the main problem for us was to find information about what it is to be gay. Who are we? Are we sick? Criminal? How should we treat ourselves? There was no one to ask.

"Nowadays, there is the internet. But through the course of my work and literary experiences, I notice that kids [still] don't have all of the information."

At the heart of the issue is the church.

The role and extent to which religion still plays a part in Russian society is contentious. Khazov-Cassia is unconvinced that the Russian Orthodox Church is as dominant as people are led to believe. While most people in the country still follow Christianity in some form, it is not a society that feels particularly religious to Khazov-Cassia. He believes it is in legislative circles where the country feels the most impact from the church.

"The orthodox church in society isn't really involved. We still have this inheritance where the country was atheist, although it is very much into the state affairs. This means it influences education and the position of politicians. If you are a minister in a small town, you have to respect the Russian Orthodox Church. You cannot speak positively about LGBT rights because you would be attacked by fellow politicians."

He does, however, say the situation is complicated. Russia's size makes it unlike many other countries where even distant communities might feel well connected.

In Russia, there is a difference between the more liberal inner cities and the rural communities – and each region can be completely unlike another.

Ninety-five per cent of people in Chechnya are Muslim, according to the 2010 census. By contrast, the region of Vologda, in western Russia, contains a population of 1.2 million people but only 0.25% are Muslim.

"Russia is huge, and we have a lot of Muslim regions. Being gay in a Muslim region is completely different from being gay, lesbian or transgender in non-Muslim regions. Muslim regions are much more conservative, and their religious leaders have more power. There, the state starts to organise campaigns against LGBT [people]. This is dangerous."

And all of this, of course, makes fiction all the more important to bridge gaps in knowledge and understanding.

Benjamin Lynch is editorial assistant at Index

ABOVE AND LEFT: Russian author Sergey Khazov-Cassia, pictured above reading extracts from his book in Soho Square, London this September

FROM THE GOSPEL ACCORDING TO

By **Sergey Khazov-Cassia**

BUNNY GOT INFECTED. The viral load isn't large enough to begin therapy yet, but he has to be registered at his parents' address back home for treatment, while making sure they don't start to suspect anything. I spent another night at his, calming him, stroking his hair, talking non-stop, kissing him, making love to him, fearlessly. Bunny was shell-shocked, but he'd already come to terms with his status and, generally speaking, he'd calmed down. I understood at once that the virus had made him mean that much more to me; I now want to care for him, get him tinned food, heat him up some milk and honey. It's just a pity we have to forget the idea of bareback sex.

Today marked three weeks and a day since I penetrated him while unprotected. I took myself to the clinic too. Usually I don't bother following the empty-stomach rule, but I decided to skip breakfast this time. It was all so familiar: roll up the sleeve, look away, clench the fist, unclench the fist, but even if (like Bunny said) in the past I'd only been 98% sure that everything was fine,

→ and that little leftover percentage hadn't worried me, today the same odds left me feeling a little less resolute.

After reaching the office I pulled up my past results to work out when my reply would come in. The emails had all arrived at different times – some at three in the afternoon, others eight in the evening. The message Bunny got saying there'd be a two-week wait for conclusive results arrived almost exactly 24 hours after the test, so I couldn't really exclude the possibility that uncertain results got sent later. The trembling had already started by midday. I couldn't tear myself away from the computer, hitting the get mail button constantly, ignoring the fact that the inbox refreshed automatically. Emails usually come in quicker on my phone, so I was keeping track there too. I'd opened the website on my phone browser so I could check the spam folder, even though I'd long since "whitelisted" the clinic's address. Oh, the forgotten feeling of vulnerable anticipation. We grown-ups live our lives in a fantasy of self-assuredness, we believe we can do anything, that no matter what happens there's always a way out – "what doesn't kill you" and all the rest. The clinic goes quiet on you, and suddenly you're thrown back to your helpless childhood. Standing paralysed in front of the plywood board that hangs on a beige university wall, where they should

We grown-ups live our lives in a fantasy of self-assuredness, we believe we can do anything

be just about to come and stick up the entrance exam results, but the secretary still won't come and there's so many surnames and the type's so small that you run your finger down the columns in spasms, and again, and again.

Or perhaps deeper, to a summer holiday outside the city, where you've stolen a ten-ruble note that smells of mothballs from under a pile of your grandma's bras, but it ripped a little in the pocket of your dirty shorts, the shop won't accept it like that, so you "swap" it over at your blind neighbour's house, in awe of your own chutzpah, and spend the money on raisin buns, which you eat in the attic and begin worrying: is the gnarled old question mark of a man going to drag himself over to complain once the forgery's been found out? What then? A beating? Grounded for a week? They'll interrogate you on where you got the money from. (After all, you can't admit to the crime, but what if they decide to count it out – does Grandma remember how much she had left of her pension?) The indulgence of the crime lies in a gamble on providence.

At two, some colleagues invited me to lunch. I didn't want to miss the email, but decided that distracting myself would be a good idea. In the cafe I was irritable, checking my phone constantly. "But look, it's not a death sentence, even if it comes back positive," I told myself. I was having difficulty believing it. Death sentence or no, it still brands you for the rest of your life, and the

expenses are enormous – we're all familiar with how accessible Russian medicine is. But no, I couldn't have got infected. I was only inside him a couple of times, a few seconds each at most, and I didn't even finish, despite how much I wanted to. Mind you, what difference does it make if I finished or not? That changes nothing.

War in Ukraine was on the menu at lunch. Larisa was recounting some gruesome news story, and our designer, Victor, was almost having an epileptic fit arguing with her. I stayed out of the conversation, tapped away on my phone, still waiting for my analysis. Larisa was sawing away at a stuffed pepper with a dull knife and talking about politicians as if she knew them all personally, and not one of them had been able to prove they were up to scratch.

"And he's the biggest Nazi of them all – that Aids-ridden paedophile. You wouldn't believe the story I watched about them last night!" She reached the crux of her argument. "If it were up to me, I'd have all of those faggots shot by firing squad."

And then... I'm not quite sure what came over me. I can hide my true self better than any Freemason, I always look for compromise, I never enter into conflict, I ignore all stones cast at me unintentionally because I'm convinced that it comes from a place not of spite, but of ignorance,

→ and who am I to judge or instruct them?

I, the calmest, most tolerant, most even-tempered person on the planet, had a sudden lapse in self-control. Lifting my eyes from the phone (still nothing) and placing my cutlery carefully, I looked at Larisa, slammed my fist on the table, and stood. The side plates screeched, some of Victor's Coke jumped from its glass, the cafe's dozens of humming voices all went quiet and turned to me. Only the Pet Shop Boys, imperturbable, carried on with To Speak Is A Sin.

"Larisa. To be honest with you, I'm sick of listening to your bullshit opinions about gays," I blurted out. "You don't understand a single thing in life, nothing whatsoever. There's not even really anything for me to say, you're just an idiot. I beg of you, keep your tongue behind your teeth when you're in my presence." By the final words I'd already started to falter, things had been going downhill since "idiot".

"What am I doing? God, what am I doing, why on earth did I do that?" I thought, trying to leave the table with some pride, but falling short.

The chairs' metallic legs were fastened together, I got caught on them and tripped, and Larisa came to her senses: "Well, isn't someone a clever boy! Don't forget to pay for your lunch, professor."

> *I, the calmest, most tolerant, most even-tempered person on the planet, had a sudden lapse in self-control*

I pulled a crumpled note jerkily from my pocket and, without waiting for change, got myself back to the office to collect my stuff and go home. My temples were throbbing, my heart pummelling my ribs. It felt like I'd just jumped out of a plane.

What had I done? What on earth had I started? Now they'll all start keeping their distance, whispering behind my back. Eventually someone'll refuse to shake my hand, then I'll get a slap in the face at the office party. Not to mention all the smirks, the tight-lipped smiles, the all-knowing, all-penetrating looks. I'll have to hand in my notice, that much is obvious. But how do I work through the next two weeks? Take my sick days? Haha. I'll just sit at home with Justin, watch his insufferable cartoons and masturbate in the toilet.

I'd completely forgotten about my results in all the hysteric chaos. Meanwhile, they'd been sent over. Negative.

Translated by **Reuben Woolley**

Sergey Khazov-Cassia *is a writer and journalist from St Petersburg. He lives in Moscow*

Banning those who ban

Jemimah Steinfeld speaks to Kuwaiti writer **Bothayna al-Essa** about overturning a ban on books in her country

49(04): 87/93 | DOI: 10.1177/0306422020981285

HERE'S A FACT about some of Kuwait's book censors: they love renowned Turkish writer Elif Shafak, who has herself been censored after she was accused of "insulting Turkishness".

"I have met many of the workers in censorship," said Kuwaiti novelist Bothayna al-Essa. "Surprisingly, many of them are passionate readers. One of them told me that they formed a book club to discuss The Forty Rules of Love by Elif Shafak.

"Some of them attend lectures of writers in my bookstore.

"I didn't understand. How can they love and ban books at the same time? We had long discussions, and I realise now that some people can't afford to be themselves fully in their jobs."

It was this revelation that forms part of al-Essa's book, Guardian of Superficialities, published in Arabic in Kuwait last September and with an exclusive English extract published here. Its premise is the overreaching censorship of literary works in Kuwait and the passage here follows a man working at the censorship bureau who is losing his mind, and potentially his marriage, due to his growing love for books which never existed before. Turns out being surrounded by great literature is not the best way to foster a hatred of it.

Al-Essa's book came out less than a year before a landmark case in the country. This August, Kuwait's government relaxed its book censorship laws in a move welcomed by writers and free speech activists. Al-Essa was one of those who led the charge.

"I worked with a group of activists to change the law by influencing parliament members," she told Index. "It was also critical to convince the government that allowing more freedom means more stability for the government and less liability on the minister. The formula worked!"

Prior to the law change, all books published in the country had to receive approval from a 12-member committee before they could be released. Offences ranging from insulting Islam to committing "immoral" acts to the page could spell the end for a book. The ministry blacklisted more than 4,000 books since 2014, including some of the world's most cherished (One Hundred Years of Solitude, by Gabriel García Márquez, for one).

For al-Essa, the author of a string of books, some of which have also been banned, literary life is now much better.

"A massacre has been stopped, finally," she said.

Censorship has defined her writing career, from the struggles to get her books published to the themes in her work.

"It made me see the dynamics of the political forces and how they affect a non-political person like me," she said. "It made me understand not only our current relationship with the state but also how it should be. It made me understand how freedom of speech is profound. It made me cherish our natural tendencies to be creative. It made me love imagination more."

TOP: The author Bothayna al-Essa, who was part of a campaign that successfully overturned book censorship in Kuwait

It made me cherish our natural tendencies to be creative. It made me love imagination more

→ Al-Essa explains that while her latest book is "fully imagined", she knows "there must be a place to store banned books somewhere in the governmental facilities. I know at some point they burn the books".

But even today, with the law relaxed, other censors are at work. Al-Essa trained as a doctor before becoming a writer and has spoken publicly about the pressures – academic and societal – to study medicine over literature (a theme featured in some of her fiction, such as All That I Want to Forget). How much pressure is there in Kuwait to conform to expectations?

"Our communities still put science on the top of the pyramid of human knowledge," she said. "People are sceptical about the 'usefulness' of literature and philosophy. There is a glamorous image that comes with being a doctor or an engineer. Most people don't really get it when they ask me, 'What do you do?', and I say, 'I write'. Because in a materialistic world, writing makes no sense.

"That's why it's more important now than it has ever been. It reminds us that we are not materialistic creatures, we are not products, not consumers. We are human beings."

Perhaps we are about to see a societal shift? Kuwait has a rich literary heritage, and the internet might be helping people celebrate this – and its current crop of writers – more. When certain apps became a vital part of our daily routines, said al-Essa, "readers, potential readers and non-readers [could] interact with writers. It changed everything". ⊗

Jemimah Steinfeld is head of content at Index

FROM GUARDIAN OF SUPERFICIALITIES

By **Bothayna al-Essa**

WHEN THE BOOK censor woke up that morning, filled with others' words, he found he had transformed into a reader.

Lying on this back, he felt a stiffness in his neck, and when he raised his head ever so slightly he could see hundreds of books surrounding his bed; books he had no recollection of bringing home. Sure, he had probably brought back one or two, but then the strangest thing happened. Overnight the books multiplied, sprouting, dividing down the middle, or copulating even. Piled up, one atop the other, forming towers leaning against his walls, hemming him in from every side.

He remembers, somewhat foggily, that the books threw his wife out. But was that yesterday or yesteryear? Her spot in their bed was empty. In the final shadows of night that veiled his memory, he recalls that she left their bed, her face red with fury, all because of a forgotten book under the covers that knocked her elbow. How accurate this was he wasn't entirely sure – more likely than not, the book had bitten her.

He doesn't remember much of what happened, akin to when an addict comes to their senses. Nighttime was the worst.

He was in the know, because of his new job, about all the maladies caused by books – in fact, he had started to display some of the symptoms: metaphors cropping up in his head; persistent ache in his upper back; snatching books involuntarily; compulsive late night reading by candlelight when the power went out. One look and it was clear he was an addict: dark circles, excessive weight loss, pallid skin, red-eyed, migraines, shoulder and neck pains, not to mention being more prone than others to all kinds of negative thoughts, as if he had been sentenced to forever seeing the glass as half full. He knew if he peeked inside his own head he'd find worry, depression, fury at the world. Of course he knew the signs, he'd personally signed the safety and security procedures compliance form.

What he does remember from last night was his wife yelling at him to choose: the books or her. With her pillow under her arm, looking at him with her bloodshot eyes, she could barely believe it when he put his hands up to his mouth and whispered: "I can't."

"You've lost your mind!" she hissed.

And then she was gone. What had happened next? What had he done the whole night? Had he slept? Had he read?

The door slamming. Left alone with the books. He had been scared, but he hadn't wanted to reveal how vulnerable he was. He knew things his wife wouldn't believe, things the other censors didn't know: books could hear, bite, multiply, copulate, establish sinister protocols to take over the world. They have a plan to colonise and conquer; word by word, poison the world with meaning. But he's meant to only skim the surface of language. He thought he had had enough training to sidestep the hazards of his job. The image of the first censor drumming the table came to mind, his words unforgettable: All language is smooth, there are no ripples. Stay on the surface, and you'll be the best censor.

He hadn't understood a whit of it. Language is smooth? What did he mean by ripples? But of late he grew to understand; he started spending the nights climbing mountains and wading through swamps, sometimes falling down holes, to the bowels of a secret world. Language was no longer just a surface. But if he shared what he thought, he'd be branded a heretic, delusional.

It all started with this one book. Terrified, he had to make sure he didn't come across as out of control. A newly appointed censor couldn't be defeated from the start. What would people say? He tried to recall last night's dream, feeling the delicate dream-like membrane of last night enveloping him like an embryo. In his dream he saw himself on an island, walking barefoot on a golden shore full of seashells, the sea roaring. He came across a discarded book in the sand. Heavy, he needed both hands to pick it up, and found beneath it a dozen tiny crabs who waved their pincers in his face. They then melted into the sand one after the other, burying themselves as if they were never there. One crab pinched his leg, waking him up to find himself in his room that was longer his room, alone in front of a beast made of countless books, a book-beast that wanted to swallow him whole.

Setting his feet on the floor, he trod on book covers that covered the surface of the world,

→ searching for empty gaps on his way to the bathroom. He extended his leg towards another gap and regained his balance with his arms out wide, waving them around as if wading through quicksand. He reached the door, opened it and poked his head through: his wife had left for work and taken the child to school. He relaxed at the thought of not having to face her that morning.

He rushed to the faucet to splash his face with water and rub his cheeks, hoping to remove the traces of the words he had read. He had changed, he had the look of a reader, as if the surface of his face had turned in on itself.

(2)

THE NEW CENSOR arrived at his office late. He had been rooted to the spot in front of the gargantuan Censorship Authority building. He had tried to guess the number of floors it had. In the elevator he had counted 30, but now he was certain, standing a few metres from the entrance, counting on his fingers, that there were, at least, six more floors.

He had heard a rumour about secret floors in government offices, they were reserved for the

---

What he does remember from last night was his wife yelling at him to choose: the books or her

---

higher-ups, filled with computers, smartphones, tablets, and there they accessed in secret what was called the internet. But they were just rumours, and he knew what sociologists said about rumours – they were the vestige of a biological instinct to invent stories, a primitive instinct from the ancient world, in the process of being wiped out.

The Censorship Authority building was a grey cube, its windows squeezed together overlooking the main road. To the side was a car park where cars could also be charged. On the left-hand side was a garden that no one paid much attention to, simply a grassy patch of land, ringed in by bougainvillea bushes and oleander. He sighed, looking intently at it all from a distance, still unbelieving of his bad luck. After long months of waiting, living on an unemployment allowance, the call came from the employment office informing him of the book censor post.

It wasn't the job that he wanted, and if he were considered good enough to work there, he would have preferred to work at the Inspection Bureau. But refusing it meant waiting for who knows how much longer, barely scraping by. He couldn't do that to his wife, who was burnt out from being the sole breadwinner. The Authority personnel in their khaki pants and standard-issue shirts were taking hurried steps to the entrance. The hallways teemed with employees; the aroma of coffee mingled with the acrid fumes of floor disinfectant. There was a thin thread of an elusive smell in the place, maybe he was the only one who had noticed it. He guessed →

→ someone had forgotten to wash his socks or that a glass of water had spilled on the carpet somewhere. Something had most certainly happened, and it was a chicken coop-boiled cabbage-damp socks smell that hung in the area. He couldn't take the matter further lest they claim he was making it up.

Even the rabbits had arrived before him. He came across two in the hallway and tried to kick them, but they were always too quick. White devils! They defecated all over the place, he had just seen three sets of droppings, at least, that had escaped the janitor's broom. To them, it seems like they were leaving behind tokens of love, in every place, cursed souvenirs to remind mankind, forgetful by nature, that their organisations were always susceptible to penetration. He yelled at the janitor to sweep up the filth. Cursing, he entered the department. He sat in his chair and instead of inspecting a book, he placed one leg atop the other and began to surveil the other seven censors.

He remembers arriving here for the first time, his appointment letter in hand. I'm the new censor, he had said. They all greeted him with a nod. Since the outset he noticed an inconceivable synchronisation in their actions; as if they were septuplets. Aside from their work uniform, they all

Whether the book was banned or permitted made no difference, what mattered was your ability to belittle the enemy

wore spectacles and were all balding. They looked like wooden dolls in a puppet theatre, invisible strings controlled by one hand, a faceless man. They would turn the page at the same time. Blink in unison. Scratch their noses at once. Stretch out their hands in one go to reach for a pen, then … suddenly start writing. They would pick up their reporting notebook and record violations from each title. Sometimes one of them would sneeze and the uniform rhythm that linked them would be disturbed. He asked himself if he too would one day be part of this collective harmony, part of their whole. But he still, until this very moment, was unable to oppose even one book.

He stared at the wall before him, at the drawn-up task schedule. The schedules updated several times in a day, so everyone knew, at any given moment, who was reading what. He thought the whole process was akin to entering a minefield or a jungle full of snakes. A rope should have been attached to each of their backs, just in case a censor lost their way back to the safe surface.

It was a large room, big enough for all of them. Each sat at his desk, and by his feet was a crate full of books awaiting inspection. Nothing eye-catching, except for the schedule on the wall: each censor had two boxes next to their name, one of the books they had finished inspecting and another for the books they were ordered to inspect. His box was empty except for one book.

It took him a while to grow familiar with the preventative measures that censors used to limit

→ the impact a book had on them. At first, he didn't quite understand and thought it was a lack of professionalism, but he soon learnt that there was a reason for everything. The first censor, for example, would intentionally cough at certain times when the room grew too quiet. He was anxious that the censors had waded too deep into the forest of language, and would lose their way back to reality. Sometimes he would sneeze, just so everyone would say "Yarhamkum Allah!", and at other times he would grumble about the heat, or anything really, to interrupt their train of thought. He also encouraged each of them to discuss what they were reading, and to swat away any intruding thoughts. The most valued behaviour was to mock what one was reading. Whether the book was banned or permitted made no difference, what mattered was your ability to belittle the enemy.

This is what happened with a poetry collection the day before. "Look here!" the second censor cried. "Listen to this:

"The sun said

"Embrace me

He thought the whole process was akin to entering a minefield or a jungle full of snakes

"And give me a drink from your forearm."

He then extended his left arm out and began to massage his forearm as if milking an udder. The censors laughed in an exaggerated manner, and took it a step further, one of them milking his toe, another pretending to pour water from his ear, and when they reached more intimate places, the first censor scolded their improper behaviour, especially with women in the building. Then it was said that one could no longer tell the difference between poetry and nonsense anymore, that literary taste was lost, to the point that everyone began wondering which poetry collection was this? After their conversation, the book lost all its worth, not just the book in question but every other book in the room. Grumbling they returned to their inspection, more wound up than they had been before.

But such tactics didn't work for him, and he didn't understand why he just couldn't, even for a moment, hate the book he held between his hands.

Translated by **Sawad Hussain**

Bothayna al-Essa *is an award-winning Kuwaiti author. She has published many novels, as well as collections of essays and children's books. She lives in Kuwait*

"Your limitless grief is a tale with no ending"

The Uighur people have a rich poetic history. Living mostly in China's north-western province of Xinjiang, many aspects of their lives have been altered by centuries of social, cultural and political change, but the importance of poetry has remained. Beautiful and lyrical, it has often reflected the pain of their persecution – persecution that has reached new heights in recent years. Here, translator **Joshua L Freeman** introduces three poets, all of whom have vanished into China's vast concentration camp network

49(04): 94/96 | DOI: 10.1177/0306422020981286

Abduqadir Jüme Tunyuquq
When novelist Mo Yan became the first Chinese citizen to win the Nobel Prize in Literature in 2012, the Chinese government was jubilant. The country's lack of Nobel winners had been a perennial topic of discussion and angst in China, so his win was celebrated extensively in the state-controlled press. Mo's books were reprinted in vast quantities throughout China, and rapidly translated into the country's minority languages. Uighur poet Abduqadir Jüme's translation of Mo's Red Sorghum hit bookstores in early 2013.

Four years later, the government sent Jüme to an internment camp. After two years there, he was transferred to a series of forced labour facilities. First he made flags, then he made earphones. More than three years have passed and Jüme is still in confinement.

As a translator of authors such as Mo, Jüme had been a bridge between Chinese and Uighur cultures. Some of his translations were commissioned by the government, but now that same government has sent Jüme and more than one million other Uighurs to a vast system of internment camps, secret prisons and forced labour facilities.

I met Jüme only a couple of times, but I was impressed by his modest, gentle manner as well as by his talent.

In addition to his work as a translator, he is a poet of considerable range, with verses ranging from lengthy post-modern works such as his Stelae of Loneliness to works with more conventional structures and themes. Since his incarceration I find myself thinking of one of Jüme's shorter, simpler poems.

ALMIKHAN'S TEARS

By ABDUQADIR JÜME TUNYUQUQ

You are the yellowed leaf of the poplar,
the tears the moon spilled to the desert sands.
Your limitless grief is a tale with no ending,
desert dreams no interpreter could understand.

When you cry, up above a star joins you in tears,
Almikhan, is that blood trickling down from your eyes?
I can't find the garden your flower grew in,
what is left after you is love's bitter demise.

The tears of Almikhan are the moon's tears,
Almikhan is a yellowing poplar leaf.
The tears of Almikhan are deeper than the ocean,
the infinite desert is the shape of her grief

In his Nobel lecture, Mo Yan remarked that "possibly because I've lived so much of my life in difficult circumstances, I think I have a more profound understanding of life. I know what real courage is, and I understand true compassion".

But Mo has not said one word about Jüme.

CULTURE

Idris Nurulla
I know Idris Nurulla from innumerable dinner parties in Ürümchi, and from afternoons I would spend with him and other friends in the wine shop where he made his living. Born in 1979, the same year as Abduqadir Jüme, Nurulla likewise made a name for himself as a poet, and especially as a translator.

The similarities between Jüme and Nurulla end there. Whereas the tall, gaunt Jüme is reserved and speaks judiciously, stocky Nurulla loves jokes and is often the life of the party. His jovial nature belies his intellectual omnivorousness and productivity. In addition to his translations of poets ranging from Baudelaire to Eliot and from Ginsberg to Amichai, in recent years Nurulla published the first full Uighur translations of Nietzsche's On the Genealogy of Morals and The Birth of Tragedy.

In 2017, as Uighurs in Ürümchi disappeared into the camps, Nurulla worried that his turn would come soon. As the proprietor of a small business he had none of the connections a position at a state workplace would have afforded him.

Nurulla was right to worry. He was detained that autumn, his wine shop boarded up. Three years later, his friends have had no news of him. This was the blank morning he wrote of a decade ago.

I AM OUTSIDE OR AT HOME

By IDRIS NURULLA

I am in a snowy morning
with the sky on my shoulders
Yesterday I walked the streets
breathing the smell of stones
drying my face on you
You're no fire, you pass by
like people pass me in the street
No one comes to my door
on a snowy morning
I am outside or at home

Nurulla was right to worry. He was detained that autumn, his wine shop boarded up

ABOVE: Kashgar old town book fair, Xinjiang

Shahip Abdusalam Nurbeg

Ten years older than Abduqadir Jüme and Idris Nurulla, Shahip Abdusalam Nurbeg grew up during the Cultural Revolution and the early reform era. After college, he began working as a middle-school teacher in his hometown, Kelpin – a position he held for three decades.

While Nurbeg was a respected teacher in Kelpin, he was known in poetic circles throughout the Uighur region as one of the most fearlessly experimental poets in the Uighur language. A charter member of the ultra-modern Nothingist school of Uighur poetry, Nurbeg was published widely in literary journals and was a mentor to young poets.

Like Jüme, Nurulla and many other Uighur poets, Nurbeg was deeply involved in translation. His crowning achievement in that field was editing Burning Wheat, the most ambitious anthology of Uighur modernist verse ever published in Chinese.

With the state vigorously pushing Uighur integration into Sinophone society, one might be forgiven for thinking that Nurbeg's translation efforts would insulate him from the mass internment of Uighur intellectuals.

His favourite poetic project was the de-construction and re-creation of Uighur poetic genres: the ghazal, the qasida (elegy or ode) and others. He delighted in flouting the rules of poetic propriety and in making new forms from fragments of old ones. He completed his magnum opus, A Thousand Elegies, not long before he was sent to the camps in mid-2017.

The last time I saw Jüme, Nurulla and Nurbeg together was in the summer of 2015. We had gone to the mountains with some other poets and translators and spent a long time one afternoon reciting poetry – their own work and poems they had translated. Among the translated verses recited that afternoon was Death Fugue, Paul Celan's poetic account of his experiences in the Nazi concentration camps.

Nurulla had translated it, and so had Perhat Tursun, another poet who has since disappeared into China's internment camps.

I don't know if Nurbeg was thinking of Celan when he wrote of black milk in A Thousand Elegies, but I can't read Nurbeg's elegies now, with their black milk from night mothers, without thinking of Celan's black milk of daybreak. I have to wonder if my friends had a premonition then that they, too, might drink the black milk.

SELECTIONS FROM A THOUSAND ELEGIES

By SHAHIP ABDUSALAM NURBEG

18
We grew the carefree evening into night
and loosed honeybees within it
Finally the bowls were filled, they overflowed
We went to drink and found the bowls were empty

308
Let's nurse from floods, we said, and went to find a mother
Said one, our night mother has black milk
Take us there, we said
Bales of orphaned evenings tumbled down

728
So fluently we stuttered
Sounds swelled with no relation to our windpipes
Oh dark where name and substance are united
We cannot call and we cannot be called

978
We were roused from wind horizons, we united
Solitary fruit was scattering without end
Look as it tumbles down
Look as we tumble down

1000
Oh anxious fruit
Watch as budding dark eternity disrobes
On one of the wayfaring nights
the bowl broke open, in its silence we arose

Translated by **Joshua L Freeman**

INDEX AROUND THE WORLD

World loses titans of free speech

Index continues to chart the attacks on journalists around the world at the same time as we mourn one of the UK's greatest, writes **Benjamin Lynch**

49(04): 97/99 | DOI: 10.1177/0306422020981287

THE WORLD OF free speech lost one of its most steadfast stewards this September when former Sunday Times editor Sir Harold Evans died at the age of 92.

Index on Censorship CEO Ruth Smeeth wrote of his contributions to the protection of free speech in the UK, saying he was: "A journalist who was fearless in challenging the establishment and shining a light on some of the most appalling scandals of his age, reinventing investigative journalism, ensuring that his work changed minds and the law. A publisher who changed the political landscape."

Evans was a patron of Index and wrote for the magazine on many occasions.

He was also one of the most admired journalists of his time, known for speaking truth to power.

His many achievements included bringing to light the thalidomide scandal in the UK. This was a drug to help with morning sickness which was routinely prescribed to pregnant women during the late 1950s and early 1960s and was found to cause a number of miscarriages, as well as birth defects.

The Sunday Times Insight team led the investigation into the scandal very much under the drive and direction of Evans. Unable to report many of the facts due to reporting restrictions, Evans eventually won a case at the European Court of Human Rights against the UK. It was a landmark moment for journalism in the country.

By this point, Evans had already risked prosecution when publishing extracts from memoirs of the recently deceased Richard Crossman, a former Labour cabinet minister. The Official Secrets Act imposed a 30-year rule on the publication of cabinet memoirs, but this is a rule which is now largely ignored – thanks in part to Evans.

We also mourned another fighter for free speech in October when news reached us that French teacher Samuel Paty had been brutally murdered outside his school merely for showing pictures from French satire magazine Charlie Hebdo. Paty was teaching his students about free expression and its importance. While never directly involved in Index, Paty was of course promoting the core values we fight for. To this extent we have written several tributes to him online and in this magazine (see p52).

RIGHT: The formidable Sir Harold Evans, former Sunday Times editor and Index patron, who passed away in September

CREDIT: David Shankbone/Wikimedia

Awards and upwards

Evans continues to remind modern audiences of the virtues of bravery and the power of words in the face of adversity and journalists, artists and activists from around the globe are being recognised for such acts. After receiving nominations for the 2021 Index awards from people across the globe, the nominations are now closed. The awards ceremony is planned for next autumn, Covid-19 depending. They have been moved from their usual date in April because Index is keen to hold the ceremony as a live event.

Senior events and partnerships manager Leah Cross said: "We have only three categories this year, which are journalism, art and campaigning."

The pandemic changed the face of several projects Index is heavily involved in. Hampered but not prevented by the pandemic was Banned Books Week, the yearly celebration of the freedom to read, which also moved its events online.

Cross said: "It was very different because we had to move to digital events instead of live events. The British Library has a great set-up for online events, so I feel it was still really interesting. It was nice to have an opportunity to attract writers from different parts of the world."

She also spoke of the importance of donations and funding which allow Index to continue to carry out its work. Index recently secured a grant from Arts Council England.

"The idea of this fund is to support charities and organisations at risk because of the current pandemic," she said. "It is a grant that will sustain us but also lead us into our 50th anniversary year, giving us a chance to reflect on the work we have done over the last 50 years.

"It will give us the chance to think about what Index wants to do in the future and where our efforts are best placed to help those persecuted."

Media violations mapped

Many of the nominations for the awards, for which donations and grants certainly help, will be reflections of courageous acts under tough conditions caused by the pandemic. Crises, both national and global, often allow governments to ramp up restrictions and clamp down on basic civil liberties. Media freedoms are no exception.

BELOW: The report of our map Disease Control, which has tracked attacks on journalists that have happened as a result of Covid-19

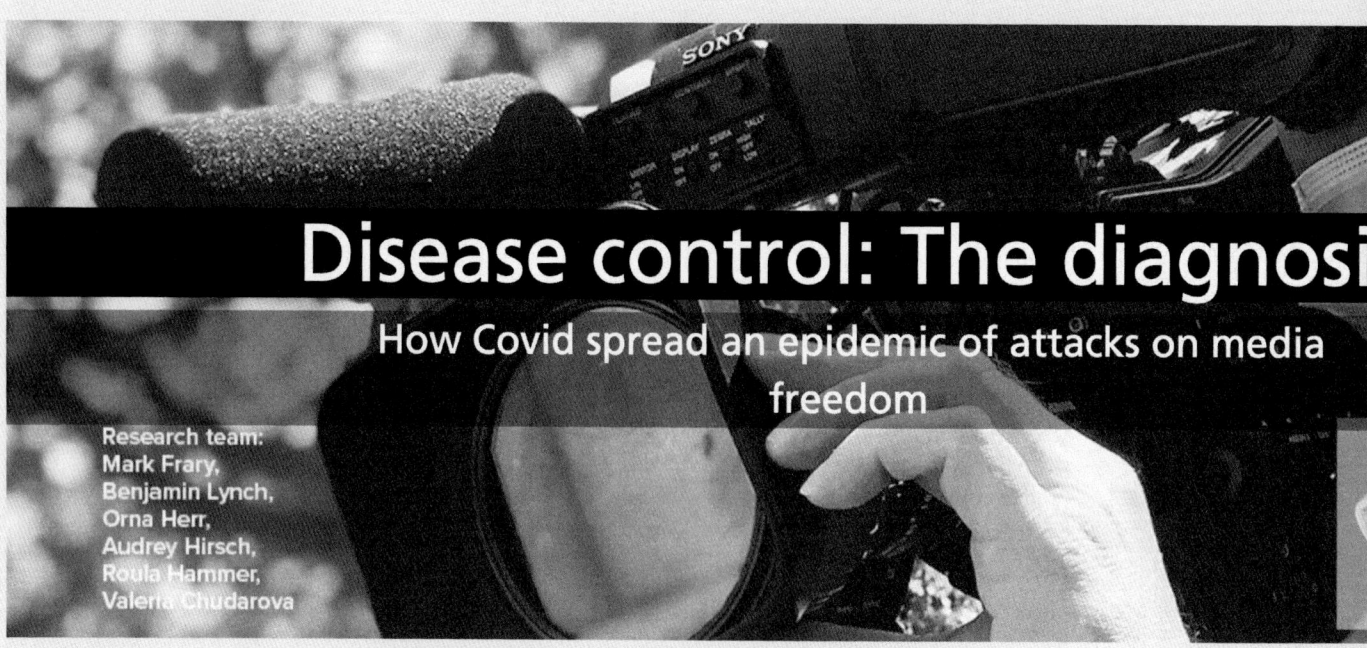

Disease control: The diagnosi
How Covid spread an epidemic of attacks on media freedom

Research team:
Mark Frary,
Benjamin Lynch,
Orna Herr,
Audrey Hirsch,
Roula Hammer,
Valeria Chudarova

CREDIT: Index on Censorship

In partnership with Justice for Journalists, Index put together an interactive map of countries using the coronavirus pandemic to introduce harmful legislation towards journalists and media outlets. Around the world, emergency legislation has been implemented, journalists have been attacked and buildings have been raided with important equipment seized.

Index associate editor Mark Frary helped to develop the map, which has so far logged 245 verified incidents around the world. The most common are cases of journalists who have been detained or arrested – currently 63.

A report on the map, published at the end of October, lays out the extent of the problem.

Frary said: "It really was a team effort. We just wanted to see if there were any sort of overarching trends that came out of it. It really showed that this is a global problem – even in northern Europe, where you would expect media freedom not to be under attack.

"It indicates our thoughts when we launched the project in that at times of crises, authoritarian governments and even non-authoritarian governments actually clamp down on media freedom. People are arrested just for telling the truth."

Slapps continue

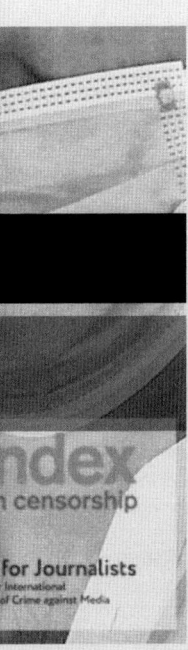

Index continues its research into the worrying trend of strategic lawsuits against public participation (Slapps), which are vexatious lawsuits that target journalists with the intent to exhaust them financially and physically.

Index first introduced a collaborative project to set out the problems with anti-media legislation in countries across Europe earlier this year. Since then, it has issued an advisory report with recommendations on how to avoid Slapps and "give journalists back their voice". In end of November it launched a toolbox to help journalists identify if they are being "Slapped". Leading the research and campaign is Index's senior policy research and advocacy adviser Jessica Ní Mhainín.

Knowledge of Slapps among the general public is still relatively low, so the likes of Ní Mhainín are attempting to change this. She expressed the importance of making the effects of the damaging legislation more widely known.

"Most people don't understand what Slapps are," she said. "Most of our work is research. We need to inform people of the need for access to information and the threat to it.

"It isn't just the threat to individual journalists; it is about the threat to the access of information and human rights defenders. We need to show that it affects people and that it affects their democracy."

Ní Mhainín believes there are positive signs that steps towards anti-Slapps legislation are being taken in EU countries. The murder of Daphne Caruana Galizia certainly drove up awareness.

In October 2017, the Maltese investigative journalist was killed by a car bomb. She had been responsible for bringing to light numerous cases of corruption by Maltese officials. Her revelations resulted in many lawsuits being brought against her in an attempt to silence her – suits which have been passed on to her living relatives.

Ní Mhainín said: "In the UK we are nowhere near [anti-Slapps legislation, so] the focus is on the EU. The Daphne Caruana Galizia cases have brought things to light. It has been useful for starting the conversation around this subject. The EU has expressed interest in imposing a directive to offer protection to journalists.

"We are trying to reach out to member states to make them understand what is happening in their own country and we are hopefully close." ⊗

Benjamin Lynch is editorial assistant at Index. He is the Tim Hetherington fellow for 2020-21

FREE THREE

Page turners or slow burners?

A review of three books published this year, all with free expression as part of their theme

49(04): 100/101 | DOI: 10.1177/0306422020981288

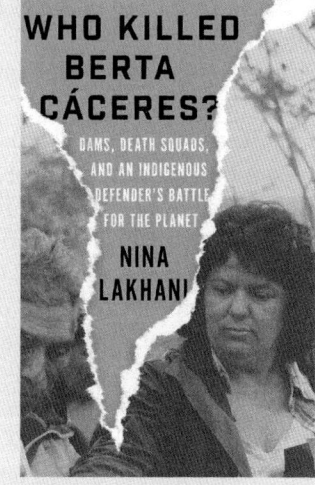

Who Killed Berta Cáceres?
Dams, Death Squads and an Indigenous Defender's Battle for the Planet

By NINA LAKHANI

WHO KILLED BERTA Cáceres? provides a detailed insight into an indigenous human rights defender's fearless pursuit of social justice in Honduras, and the extent of the corruption and collusion that led to her brutal death. In her final years, Cáceres became increasingly aware that her opposition to the construction of a hydroelectric dam was putting her life in danger. "The army has an assassination list of sixteen wanted human rights defenders, with my name at the top. I want to live, there are many things I still want to do in this world. I take precautions, but in the end, in this country where there is total impunity, I am vulnerable. When they want to kill me, they will do it," she told Nina Lakhani in 2013, three years before she was murdered.

Through Lakhani's extensive interviews, readers come to know Cáceres and to understand what made her such a relentless force for justice. "She never censored the truth, but always believed in change," said Gustavo Castro, a friend who was with Cáceres when she was killed. By her own admission, she was the product of her vocal and strong-willed foremothers. "I am basically repeating what my mother and grandmother did to fight oppression," Cáceres told Lakhani.

The author threads in the particular challenges Cáceres faced as a human rights defender in a society where women do not typically take on leadership or political roles. According to one interviewee, Cáceres "was criticised for neglecting her children, for choosing la lucha, the struggle, over motherhood". Another said they "killed her for being a woman".

In the first half of the book, Lakhani tries to put her struggle in a historical and international context. This is useful in theory but, due to the complexity, we end up jumping back and forth in time and place, which stunts the flow. Still, this context is important to understand the extent to which international greed had a role to play.

Despite the best efforts of Cáceres's family and community alongside various activists, the Honduran government has faced no significant consequences for its role in her death. Lakhani communicates the injustice through her thorough account of a compromised trial that saw seven people – but not the more powerful masterminds – convicted and sentenced. "Our battle for dignity, truth and justice does not end here," Cáceres's daughter Laura Zúñiga says in the final lines of the book. "We will keep fighting – just like Berta Cáceres did."

Overall, this is a worthwhile read, if best suited to readers with some prior knowledge of the case.

Reviewed by JESSICA NÍ MHAINÍN

BOOK REVIEW

Eat the Buddha: The Story of Modern Tibet through the People of One Town

By BARBARA DEMICK

AT THE TIME of publication, some 156 Tibetans have set themselves on fire, calling for the return of the Dalai Lama from exile in India. A third of these have come from Ngaba, in China's north-western Sichuan Province, which provides the backdrop for Barbara Demick's Eat the Buddha, a detailed and insightful account of a region which has gained the gruesome reputation of the "undisputed world capital of self-immolations".

The relationship between Tibet and the Chinese Communist Party is rarely fully witnessed by outsiders. Foreigners need special permission to enter, which is rarely granted to journalists — a testament to the difficulties faced by Demick in order to write this book.

Despite this, Demick's vivid and nuanced account of the history of the region, told through the stories of those who have experienced it, picks apart this fraught relationship. Demick has pieced together a dense and intimate account of life in Tibet and how this extreme form of activism grossly contradicts Beijing's claims that Tibetans are happy under Chinese rule.

Although the rise of the CCP is a firm feature of the backdrop of Demick's narrative, she is not as concerned with artefact or report as she is with telling personal stories of those who lived through the events of the last century. Here, Demick injects an impressive amount of detail, tracing the family histories of those both living in and exiled from the region. She expertly weaves the histories of a small number of characters — from the daughter of the last Mei king to a young Tibetan monk — with the history of the region and how it has been impacted by modern China.

Self-immolation is strictly taboo for Buddhists, and many of Ngaba's residents are ambivalent towards this form of activism. There are also residents who appreciate the infrastructure the party has brought to the region. But Tibetans are seeing more and more inequality between themselves and the dominant Han Chinese, alongside a stifling of culture, language, religion and freedom of expression — not unlike that experienced by other oppressed minorities.

Just as the self-immolators are motivated by an inability to speak up — to practise their culture and see the Dalai Lama return to Tibet — Demick seeks to give them a voice.

Reviewed by LEAH CROSS

Homeland Elegies

By AYAD AKHTAR

THIS IS A work of "autofiction", a somewhat nebulous term. It certainly reads like a memoir, only the characters' names have been changed to preserve their identities. Predictably, the book falls between the two stools of truth and fiction.

It has an intriguing framing. A Pulitzer Prize-winning playwright writes a post-9/11 stage-play in which two of the characters exhibit empathy for the terrorists. The plot echoes Ayad's own life, who was asked whether he felt empathy following his play and said he felt that was not the right question to ask an artist. As momentum built behind Donald Trump in 2016, media outlets again called Ayad asking him whether all American Muslims felt that way. This book is therefore a sort of response. Only it never really fulfils that function.

It's a touching study of Ayad's relationship with his immigrant father, a heart surgeon who assimilates very quickly to US values but who will never be completely integrated. It's a less touching study of Ayad's relationship with the love of his life, whose simultaneous relationships with Ayad and a white man ultimately lands all three with syphilis. The three consequently go their separate ways and Ayad is then utterly blindsided when his love has an arranged marriage back in Pakistan.

This lack of insight in Ayad is a recurrent theme. One might find it endearingly honest, but it doesn't speak well of a playwright who is supposed to be a consummate observer of human beings. Ayad doesn't know that his father slept with prostitutes; It's only after his mother's death that he finds out she had an unrequited love who was killed in Pakistan by the CIA; Speaking to his father on election night, Ayad is seething because he believes he voted for Trump, but doesn't ask him.

These are all interesting dynamics, but the Ayad of the book – and therefore the Ayad Akhtar who created him – are poor guides into them. The book is best when two of his mentors, an Asian hedge fund manager and a black film producer, explain the underlying economics of the USA to him, and in doing so we get an insight into how society embraced Trump.

It ends with a postscript about Ayad being no-platformed by a college Muslim society because it didn't approve of his Muslim stereotypes, but it soon changes its stance when a group on the right objects to Ayad's supposed sympathy for terrorists. It's a suitable postscript in that one is none the wiser for the experience of reading this book.

Reviewed by MARC NASH

END NOTE

Fighting for Covid information

Access to reliable information is more important than ever during a global pandemic. **Lauren Brown** looks at the people who are working hard to ensure that even those in the most censored settings receive it

THE SPRAWLING COX'S Bazar, in the south-east of Bangladesh on the border with Burma, is – according to the UN Population Fund – the most densely populated refugee camp in the world.

It comprises 34 settlements spread over almost 7,000 acres and houses about 40,000 people per square kilometre. Many live in makeshift tarpaulin and bamboo shelters. The majority of the population arrived three years ago when, in August 2017, more than 740,000 Rohingya fled violence and persecution in Burma. It's believed it is now home to 860,000 refugees.

An outbreak of Covid-19 would be devastating. Accessing healthcare was already difficult, with language barriers and a lack of information complicating access, so many people relied on the internet. That changed in September 2019 when 3G and 4G services were shut off in the camps by the Bangladesh Telecommunication Regulatory Commission, ostensibly to curtail crime. The pandemic threw the potentially catastrophic implications of such a move into sharp relief.

"When we didn't have internet access, it was a very difficult time for us and very difficult to get information, specifically about Covid-19," Shamima Bibi, a 30-year-old resident of Cox's Bazar, told Index.

The internet has since returned, in part due to pressure from people. But there are reports that it is still patchy at best and fears that it might be cut off once again.

"I believe information is basic aid but we didn't get this aid for many months and had to suffer very hard to get information. Nowadays, many youths are learning from the internet where before our youths didn't get any opportunity to learn education at school or university. They are always trying to learn basic education from the internet, so when we lost the internet at that time many people lost hope," said Bibi.

Muzibur Rahman, another 30-year-old refugee, told Amnesty International at the time: "The world is passing a hard time because of the Covid-19 pandemic and we the Rohingya are in a difficult situation because we cannot get timely updates about health and safety measures."

Felicia Anthonio, lead campaigner on digital advocacy group Access Now's #KeepItOn campaign, believes "network disruptions violate human rights" and is working to ensure all victims of internet shutdowns or subtler "speed-throttling" moves – in Cox's Bazar and beyond – aren't left in the dark.

"Around the globe, the outbreak of Covid-19 has underscored the importance of the internet and digital communications tools in advancing access to timely, reliable and accurate information during crises," she said. "The internet shutdowns and throttling at Cox's Bazar placed some of the world's most at-risk people in more extreme, dire circumstances. With no access to information about the virus — or its mitigation — the government of Bangladesh endangered lives."

The #KeepItOn campaign is amplifying the impact of internet shutdowns on human rights

with the Shutdown Story project and a podcast series, Kill Switch, in order to put pressure on the relevant actors to take action.

Though the internet switch-off predates Covid-19, the results made the difficult lives of Rohingya refugees even more so. And while the Bangladeshi government restored connection to the camps in August, the impact during the pandemic cannot be overstated.

The situation at Cox's Bazar is just one example of censorship inhibiting the dissemination of accurate Covid-19 information. In some historically repressive states, the virus has provided an excuse for accelerated repression. Prayut Chan-o-cha, prime minister of Thailand, issued an emergency decree in March restricting freedom of speech on the basis of stopping "dangerous rumours" about Covid-19.

China has also tightened restrictions, with critics of the government's handling of the pandemic "reprimanded". Citizen journalist Chen Qiushi might be facing up to five years in jail, while others have received police warnings.

Amnesty researcher Kai Ong said that while

> *To bypass censors, users started using acronyms and codewords, from basic ones such as "wh" and "hb" for Wuhan and Hubei*

the Chinese government's silencing of dissenting voices began long before the outbreak, since then "the government has been trying to control the circulation of information and build a narrative that hides [its] wrongdoing".

Resourceful citizens have nevertheless found ways of getting around China's Great Firewall. Thousands without access to Twitter, Facebook and other social media channels turned to GitHub, the world's largest open-source software site, to share information and memories. One collaborative repository named #2020nCovMemory included personal accounts of the tragedy, as well as investigative reports. Similarly,

> *There are no independent media outlets in Iran and no such thing as freedom of the press, so many people don't trust the official information*

→ 2020nCov_individual_archives included accounts of life during the pandemic. The creators of the former took it down amid fears for their own safety, but the latter remains live.

On Weibo, one of the biggest social media platforms in China, users started noticing as early as February that certain words were being restricted – most notably "Wuhan" and "Hubei", the source of the outbreak. The government's handling of the crisis and the initial cover-up of the epidemic fuelled public criticism, and legions of online censors began monitoring coronavirus content. A report from Citizen Lab found that on WeChat, combinations such as "Xi Jinping goes to Wuhan" and "Wuhan + CCP + Crisis + Beijing" were being routinely blocked.

To bypass censors, users started using abbreviations, acronyms and codewords, from basic ones such as "wh" and "hb" for Wuhan and Hubei to more complicated substitutions such as "F4", a name taken from a Taiwanese boy band from the 2000s that now refers to four regional politicians – the governor of Hubei, the secretary of the province's Communist Party committee, the mayor of Wuhan and the party secretary of Wuhan.

Kai said: "Netizens use acronyms to circumvent censorship of sensitive words – for example, 'ZF' for zhengfu (government) – and they also rotate and distort pictures to dodge image censors."

But he believes that this cat-and-mouse game is unsustainable and is a double-edged sword. "These tactics may have delayed the content being censored. However, these cryptic languages hinder the dissemination of these messages online," he said.

After China, Iran is one of the countries most affected by censorship during the pandemic.

In the 2020 Reporters Without Borders (RSF) World Press Freedom Index, Iran was ranked as "one of the most oppressive countries", at 173 out of 180 (China came in at 177). According to RSF, the state does "not hesitate to harass journalists in order to suppress news and information that embarrasses the regime".

"There are no independent media outlets in Iran and no such thing as freedom of the press, so many people don't trust the official information and numbers provided on Covid-19 as well as other topics," said Yalda Zarbakhch, a German-Iranian journalist at Deutsche Welle. "[People] are longing for unbiased information on the pandemic and its effects."

She and colleague Oliver Linow, chief of internet circumvention activities at Deutsche Welle, decided to provide Iranians with just that. They turned their attention to Psiphon, a tool already widely used in Iran that provides uncensored access to the internet. A website that collated information from multiple sources was launched in March in Farsi and made available for free. A Mandarin version has now also been set up.

In an increasingly technological world, it makes sense that circumvention efforts have centred on open-source platforms such as GitHub – tools that bypass state censors and 3G and 4G access as in the case of Cox's Bazar. With the hope of vaccinations on the horizon, the Deutsche Welle team anticipates an even greater need for free and accurate information over the coming months, and it intends to be prepared.

"When the first vaccines are made available, people will have a great need for information during this phase," said Linow. "So we are considering expanding the campaign to more countries next year.

"We know that we cannot stop the evolution of increasing censorship on the internet. But at least we can bring sleepless nights to autocrats and reach people who find it difficult or impossible to get unbiased information." ⊗

Lauren Brown *is a freelance journalist based in the UK*